NORTH
BEACH
DIET

KIM BAILEY

Foreword By

Ophelia Belly & Chuck Roast

RUTLEDGE HILL PRESS
NASHVILLE, TENNESSEE

A DIVISION OF THOMAS NELSON, INC.
WWW.THOMASNELSON.COM

A portion of the profits from the sale of each book goes to the Science and Health Research Institute in Tri-Star, Colorado: monies directed to Florida Laboratory for Adolescent Behavior (FLAB).

This book is written and published solely for its humor value, and you should always consult with your doctor before starting a new diet program.

Rutledge Hill Press books may be purchased in bulk for educational, business, fundraising, or sales promotional use. For information, please email SpecialMarkets@ThomasNelson.com.

Published by Rutledge Hill Press, a Division of Thomas Nelson, Inc., P.O. Box 141000, Nashville, Tennessee, 37214.

Library of Congress Cataloging-in-Publication Data Available

1-4016-0216-9

Printed in the United States of America
05 06 07 08 09—5 4 3 2 1

ADDITIONAL BOOKS BY THE AUTHOR

• COMING SOON •

The DaVinci Diet

The murder of the personal chef for the curator of the Louvre leads to a trail of clues involving the low-carb diet and how it may have played a role in the death of Mona Lisa.

The Purpose-less Driven Life

Man's search for meaning is endless. The author explores his compelling journey for boundless life through good food.

A Children's Classic
Of Course I'll Eat Green Eggs and Ham

I will eat them in a box, or with a fox, in a house, or with a mouse. Your child will be enchanted by the tales of Jumbo, Dumbo, and Louie, on their quest to find the ultimate Green Eggs and Ham.

TABLE OF CONTENTS

Acknowledgments vii
Foreword ix

PART I – GETTING STARTED

Chapter 1 What This Diet Can Do for You 1
Chapter 2 The Smart Start: Our Seven-Day 25
Quick-Gorge Program
Chapter 3 The Slow Start: Let Your Fork Point North 31

PART II – ROBUST GOURMET

Chapter 4 Gaining Weight Has Never Tasted So Good 37
Chapter 5 Our Sandwich Bar 77
Chapter 6 Vegetables: How They Should be Eaten! 83
Chapter 7 The Main Course 99
Chapter 8 When You're Home Alone 111

PART III – LIVING THE NORTH BEACH WAY

Chapter 9 Everyday Life on the North Beach Diet 121
Chapter 10 Virtual Exercise: Good for Mind and Body 131
Chapter 11 Journaling: Your Key to Success 139

Index 161
About the Author 165

ACKNOWLEDGMENTS

There are two people who, without their help and support, this book would never have been written. They have encouraged me and stood by my life's journey every step of the way.

The loves of my life: Sara Lee and Little Debbie.

They stuck with me throughout my formative years, through thick and thin. College exams would never have been passed without them. The three of us were inseparable during those all-night last-minute cram sessions. And life, well, it just wouldn't have been the same without these two sweeties.

Both in my personal or professional life, when I was stressed, they were always there. When I was happy, I reached for them . . . the closer we became, the more my contentment grew. Yes, sadly, there were times when I pushed them away for some sweet thing dressed up in pink, blue, or yellow—but they were tarts, unable to satisfy my real needs.

So my loves, it is with true fondness, care, and devotion, that I dedicate this revolutionary new program to you. You've found the way to my heart . . . you have no Equal.

KB

Foreword

THE POSSIBLE DREAM

Welcome to *The North Beach Diet*! And a hearty congratulations for taking this initial step to improving your overall quality of life. You will find no other diet approach that will allow you to gain weight faster than this unique program. And think about it, you can literally be two sizes bigger in just one weekend . . . just by following the easy "Eat-Till-You-Drop" system.

We are so proud of our great friend Kim Bailey who gained 145 pounds in just six months, became emotionally insulated, and allowed food to control every aspect of his life—and with this sound program now you can too.

Have you ever fantasized about eating anything and everything you ever wanted? Have you wondered what it would be like to wear muumuus all day long, or fit into size 54 pants? Do you dream about what it would be like to be ogled admiringly by people as you sashay down the beach with a giant-size bag of Nutter Butters in one hand, and a large Frosty in the other? Dream no more—it's all possible with the incredible fat-track program.

You will never again have to eat fruits, unless they are baked in a cobbler or pie and topped with lots of rich ice cream and caramel, or vegetables without buttered bread crumbs and cheddar cheese sauce. No more broiled, steamed, baked, anything . . . it's fried all the way, baby, from this point forward, and fried as everything should be—in great-tasting lard.

Just think, tonight after dinner, you can have a two-vegetable snack of french fries and ketchup; and wash it all down with a hearty root beer vanilla ice cream float. Think about how much fun your entire family will have, watching TV passing around a can of Redi-Whip topping—squirting it in each other's mouths, seeing who can swallow the most in one never-ending spray. Yes, it's a program for the entire family.

Even the "Virtual Exercise" plan is simple and fun to follow. You'll be "Relaxin' to the Oldies" in no time. Remember, there are no foods you can't eat—throw out discipline, moderation, and portion control! Eat as much as you can hold—then, a little bit more. Every day is like Thanksgiving Day on the North Beach Diet. The dream is possible. Enjoy!

Ophelia Belly
and Chuck Roast
2005

PART I
GETTING STARTED

Chapter One

WHAT THIS DIET CAN DO FOR YOU

If you are like me, in the past, I'd buy or join a new weight gain program and go right to what I could eat. Often I wouldn't even read the program; and when I did, I wouldn't follow it. Since I'd been on so many programs, I knew all the answers and was interested only in the "quick fix."

If someone told me that I'd have to plan my eating, "Go fly a kite" would be my typical response, for I knew all the answers. I'd start a new program time and again and do the same thing over and over, expecting different results. Now how crazy is that? Can you identify with me? I bet you can.

Today is the time to change. Not tomorrow. Start now. We've all played the "if only" game far too many times. Forget the past, or at least vow not to repeat it. Before you begin, however, there are a few things you should do to better guarantee your success these next thirty days. In order of importance, they are:

1. Read the whole thing. Read the entire program, page by page, at least once before you begin. Complete the Support Journal daily, for the next thirty days.

2. Find some partners. Find three chubby accountability partners to follow this program with you for the next thirty days. Find like-minded people who need to gain approximately the same amount of weight and are close to the same non-athletic level as you. Make sure they are just as committed to following this program.

Family, friends, and business associates are the best source, but if no one is available, distribute flyers in your neighborhood (much like a yard sale) or put a small classified ad in your local paper. Here is a sample ad:

GAIN WEIGHT, 30-DAY PROGRAM
Female (or male) Fat Partner wanted for eating,
weigh-ins & holding each other accountable.

Mention the area of town you live in because you want people close by for the convenience of meeting daily for Virtual Exercise. Also, make sure they invest in this program, just as you did. This is important because you want them to take it seriously. If you can only find one or two others, that's okay, but we've found that a group of four is best. If you can find no one, go ahead and follow the program solo but keep looking. Having a partner or two will increase your chances of success significantly.

3. *Review menus.* As we've discussed, if you eat out a lot, get menus from local restaurants you frequent and review them to determine the highest calorie items on the menu, so you can decide what to order in advance. If they serve large portions, make sure they will accommodate you by serving at least twice as much of the high carbohydrate foods such as corn and potatoes. If you cannot finish all the food, put the remaining in a take-out container and try to eat it on the way home.

4. *Plan meals in advance.* Plan every single meal you are going to cook and eat, at home or not, in the office or out, seven days in advance. Carry high-fat, high-calorie snack foods (preferably Little Debbie's, Sara Lee, or Hostess) with you everywhere. Go no place without snack food nearby. Don't ever get caught off guard. It's in your control.

5. *Curtail that exercise.* Most people think that exercise gives them a license to eat more. It's true. I've seen so many people become disillusioned by exercising diligently and not gain any weight, or worse, lose weight. They just didn't increase their eating to a level outweighing the expenditure of calories. If you are serious about gaining weight, you've got to expand your portion sizes, and stop walking.

6. *Keep a journal.* Keeping a journal is a great way for you to get in touch with the emotions of why you eat the way you eat. Knowledge is power and understanding what stresses and motivates you will help

SING
TO WIN A
CRUISE

VIDEO TAPE FOOD JINGLE CONTEST

Win A 7-Day "All You Can Eat"
Luxurious Cruise Including Airfare*

THAT'S RIGHT, you can win a 7-day "all you can eat," luxurious cruise for two, including airfare, just by sending in a video tape of you (and others if you wish) singing all, or any one of the well-known food company jingles below.

It's got to be sung in the company's tune. Wear a costume if you'd like. Sing in falsetto, operatic, or just your normal every day singing voice—sing it straight, or sing it funny—sing it with a friend, a group, or by yourself . . . you make the call. Sing the lyrics to the jingles listed or any other food jingle you can remember. (For complete lyrics visit website below.)

Remember These Favorites? Sing-It-Proud & Send Us A Video Tape.

Oscar Mayer Weiner and Balogna songs

Everybody doesn't like . . . what? Sara Lee

What kind of kids like Armor Hot Dogs?

Chili's Baby Back Ribs

What Does Burger King "hold" on their song?

Can you sing the Frito Bandito theme?

What's the Chiquita Banana lady say?

Do you think Campbell Soup is . . . Good?

Are you havin' Beef-A-Ro-neeeeeeeee tonight?

Do you really deserve a break today . . . at where?

Aunt Jemima Pancakes without her what, is like what?

What city is like a Rice-A-Roni treat?

SEND ALL ENTRIES TO:
NORTH BEACH DIET—FOOD JINGLE CONTEST
POST OFFICE BOX 14304
TAMPA, FLORIDA 33629

For complete details and restrictions, visit
www.northbeachdietonline.com

reshape your day and consequently reshape your body to a new, much rounder you.

Short-Term Thinking for Long-Term Results

In addition to journaling and maintaining a log of your eating, there are other formulas guaranteed to produce success in your desire to gain weight. And they are not at all difficult to follow. We are not telling you that to be successful you will have to do everything we suggest. You can be assured of one thing, however: The more closely you follow the program, the more weight you'll gain in the shortest amount of time.

Be assured too, that if by this time next year you are ten pounds more than you are now, that is success, especially if your history is losing or staying the same weight year after year. When reading this section, an OB-GYN doctor friend of mine, Dr. Mark Cooper, suggested that most people who need to gain a great deal of weight (including me) would not view a ten-pound weight gain in a year as success. I agreed, even though I'd like to think I would.

What I'm trying to get to here is if we are trying to gain too much too quickly, we often will not be successful unless bingeing methods are imposed. I've done that too, and sometimes it works, but often it doesn't work for the long term. Whether it's a hundred pounds a year or ten, the true measure of success should be if you met the goal you established for yourself and if you feel comfortable with that benchmark and your effort. If not, do something different, such as following our program.

The best way to gain weight is to eat massive amounts of food constantly throughout the day, without binge eating.

Too often we are inflexible and rigid in our demands for immediate weight gain. Hence, we fail because we feel we failed, so we say, "Aw, the heck with it." That thinking, my friends, is "stinkin'-thinkin'," to quote a not-so-close friend of mine.

What is a realistic weight gain goal for you? Write it down. Be realistic and think short term. For the next thirty days what would you like to accomplish? Answer the following questions:

- How much weight do I want to gain in thirty days?
- Is this a realistic goal?

- What is my realistic Virtual Exercise goal?
- Is this a realistic goal?
- What obstacles could challenge me in achieving my goal?
- What is my plan when I am faced with these obstacles?

You'll notice that we didn't ask how much weight you wanted to gain overall. Begin to think in thirty-day spans (even in seven-day spans), and one day at a time in that thirty-day period. I would often say my goal is to gain a hundred pounds. No time frame, but just as quickly as I could. There should be no surprise that failure was on the horizon. When I began to think short-term, the struggle seemed much less daunting, much more achievable.

Gaining two or three pounds a week, eight to twelve pounds in thirty days: Is that possible for you? Or are you trying to gain thirty pounds in thirty days for some special event? If so, this is not the program for you. Become a short-term thinker for long-term results.

If you really follow our suggestions, the first week a woman on our meal plan will probably gain ten pounds and a man will gain twenty. It takes women longer to gain real fat weight—often, much of their gain is water-weight. So take that into consideration as you set your goal. If your goal is to gain ten pounds in thirty days, but you know you're going to gain half of that, or more, in the first seven days, adjust your goal if you wish. Think it through, and be realistic.

In a Single Day You Get
86,400 Seconds
1,440 Minutes
And 24 Hours
Make Every One of Them Count

Plan, Focus, Then Execute

This program can be just what you've been looking for. Do you have trouble believing that it can work for you? Can't quite summon the enthusiasm to start yet again on your goal toward lasting weight gain? Read on for tips to help you throughout the program.

Throw Away Your Thigh Master, Kiss Suzanne Somers Goodbye!

SAY HELLO TO THE

FLAB-MASTER

Designed with the Conscientious Virtual Exerciser in Mind

Our cracker-jack team of fitness experts led by internationally known fitness guru Dan Wall has developed a piece of equipment to make all other health gear obsolete.

It May Look Like Just a Bag of Double-Stuffed Oreo Cookies But It's Much, Much, More.

In scientific studies conducted at the nuclear testing plant in Los Alamos, New Mexico, adipose tissue on both thighs was increased by a staggering 33.6 percent in just two weeks by using this product.

30-Minute Money Back Guarantee
ORDER TODAY!

As a special bonus for ordering now, you'll receive a 12-foot body measuring tape just for trying the Flab-Master. And if you return this product for any reason, you may keep the body measuring tape as our free gift to you.

For overnight delivery visit our website:
www.northbeachdietonline.com

$14.95
plus $3.56 S&H

DINER'S CLUB CARD Only Please

Void Where Prohibited By Law

Have You Lost Hope?

Have you lost hope of ever finding a solution to your battles with weight gain? All of us have lost hope at one point or another. In this program, countless people have found the hope needed to propel and motivate them to change—to make lasting significant weight gain. You can too. The time to begin is now.

But to succeed you must begin to think differently about yourself, and you must begin to think differently about food. You must begin to think differently about exercise as well. New rituals need to replace the old ones. To think and act differently, you must develop positive mental tapes to replace the current negative ones you play over and over again in your mind.

Has weight loss controlled you? Has being thin kept you from achieving your life goals? If so, close your eyes and visualize yourself at three hundred pounds, rolling around the living room floor with your kids, having strangers show little acts of kindness by helping you out of your mini-van. Visualize the new you daily, hourly, until those negative tapes are replaced forever. Success breeds success. Make visualization a ritual. Success will come, and hope will spring forth once again.

Motivation for Change

What's your motivation for choosing our program? Is it a reunion, a wedding, a cruise, a vacation, or even an anniversary? Whatever your motivation, do it for *you*. "Living large" no longer has to be a slogan. Think of our program as a new way of life—one day at a time—not just a way to get you to a larger size for some special event, then trimming back down afterward. That was your old way. Today, right now, you're going to start thinking differently about food. Food is your friend, your companion, your new social outlet . . . you'll never have to be alone again.

Feel Dynamic in Just Seven Days

Our Seven-Day Quick-Gorge Program is designed to jump-start you to success in breaking the habit of consuming fruits and vegetables without sugar and butter. By following our innovative step-by-step approach to food and virtual exercise, you'll feel absolutely dynamic in just seven short days. Think about it: You've been the giver all your life. Now you'll force people to give to you. They'll be the ones stooping over to pick up your car keys and lifting you in and out of your car.

And if you have a lot of weight to gain like I did (I gained 145 pounds on this exact same program), the safe quick weight gain you'll experience the first seven days will catapult you into a new way of thinking about food for long-term success. You'll be somebody to reckon with in no time. No one will be able to push you around any-more . . . literally.

Our awesome tasting recipes in the Robust Gourmet section are designed to take you from day eight to the hefty self-indulgent body you always desired. Robust Gourmet excludes no food. If you want a piece of chocolate cake, enjoy it! But don't stop at one piece; eat the whole darn cake—and throw in a half gallon of ice cream. Robust Gourmet will provide you with literally dozens of great-tasting recipes, testimonials, and easy-to-follow tips allowing you to change negative eating patterns for life. No longer will high-fat, high-sugar, great-tast-ing foods be the enemy. With Robust Gourmet, food becomes your best friend.

Been There—Done That

Sometimes it just helps to know that you aren't alone. Countless millions have felt your frustration, anger, and hurt. Millions have strug-gled with seemingly unconquerable obsessions to lose weight. I have walked the same road. Here is my story.

Weight has always been an issue for me. As far back as my mind's eye extends I was lean, thin, slight, and gaunt. In my fam-ily, I was taunted as the "athletic one," as if I wasn't good enough for the rest of them.

It seemed as though my metabolism ran too fast for fat tissue to adhere to my lanky frame. I was adiposely challenged. My mom would bring platters of spaghetti and meatballs to the table—but no matter how much I ate, it was never enough to gain blubber mass. My brothers and sisters would gain all the weight . . . it was truly a difficult time for me.

My parents met with the administrators of my junior high school to try and figure out the problem. After a few weeks of observation, they discovered that I traded my peanut butter clusters and Fritos for apples and oranges. For some reason I just liked fruit.

After much counseling and advice seeking, my mom and dad developed a plan of action, which excluded sports and included a great deal of television watching. My new plan was to return home from school and immediately sit in front of the TV and snack until dinner. Admittedly, at first, it was tough—I wanted to be out running, jumping, and playing with the other kids in my neighborhood.

WARNING!
Doing this program alone can be hazardous to your weight gain. Find three hefty accountability and support partners before you begin.

But after only a few short weeks of lying in front of our large-screen Panasonic, dunking my Cheetos in Dr. Pepper and ice cream, my new regimen paid off. My stomach began to hang over my belt . . . just a bit at first, but by tenth grade, I was up to 260 pounds. My parents were so proud. Admittedly, I was too. Finally I fit in.

You may very well guess what happened with my children. My youngest son Buddy exhibited some of the same habits that I did as a child. You know what they say, "The chips don't fall too far from the bag." Buddy was a fast swimmer, and even made the swim team—his mother and I were worried. Buddy and I began to spend more time together as I coached him in some of my old tricks from my youth, such as using heavy cream instead of milk to make milkshakes. It was a bonding time for us both.

We soon hit pay dirt when we invested in a Play Station. Now he never moves from the video screen. You parents—if you find your kid playing sports all the time, our hearts go out to you. My advice is to cheese nip it in the bud as soon as possible.

Now, instead of swimming, Buddy wades in the shallow end of the pool. And you know what? He's the team manager.

My struggle with weight has left scars that run clear to my soul.

It also has given me a great compassion for others, an intolerance for prejudice (even against thin people), and a tremendous appreciation for life's little joys . . . like a warm homemade carrot cake, topped with macadamia nut ice cream, hot fudge, Marshmallow Fluff, Cool Whip, and chocolate sprinkles (recipe on page 51).

In life, we have many choices. I choose not to be that skinny, underweight, sports-minded athlete anymore. I choose to seize each day and make weight gain my own. I choose to live my life as intended—stuffed and happy—and I invite you to join me.

Get Rid of the On/Off Mentality

When you undereat one day, try not to beat yourself up by saying, "Aw, the heck with it—I've really screwed up, so I might as well eat light for the rest of the day and start again tomorrow." Snap out of it—immediately drive (don't walk, even if it's next door) to the nearest convenience store and buy a Baby Ruth candy bar—the nuts combined with chocolate and the gooey caramel center make a great remotivator.

What makes the Tower of Pisa lean? . . . It never eats!

Babe Ruth (the overweight baseball player, not the candy bar) struck out more than he hit. But he never quit. He kept getting up to bat and became the giant of baseball . . . and he could really pack away the steak and potatoes.

Begin to think of a poor food choice (such as fresh fruits and vegetables), or going bike riding or swimming as just wandering off course—not off the program. View this program as a journey, a journey to a new you. The on/off mentality creates an all-or-nothing thought process.

Airplane pilots are trained to make mild adjustments when they wander off course, which happens often, believe it or not. If they correct too hard or too fast, perilous effects can be triggered. The same can be true with your diet. Many people may very well skip a meal when they eat too much. That's not the North Beach way. *Never skip a meal.* If you've eaten too little at a meal, it's okay; at least you've eaten. Pat yourself on the back and go a little heavier at the next meal. That's the way you train yourself to keep eating, even when you don't feel like it. So when you wander off course a bit or even a lot, don't beat yourself up.

Just wander back—you'll find that sweets help you get right back on your program.

Always Use Food as an Emotional Outlet

Let me say it loud and clear: "*Food* is by far the *best friend* you'll ever have." What's the first thing that happens when a death in the family occurs? People bring us food. What do we do after the funeral? People come to the house and eat. When you move to a new neighborhood, what do your neighbors bring you? Food. When little Susie gets an A on her report card, you celebrate, with—what else? Food!

All our holidays are centered around food, as they should be. In most homes, our religious faith takes a backseat to our holiday dinner. On Christmas, for example, our family goes to church early Christmas eve night so we can come back and eat, and then have the entire day on Christmas left to celebrate with—what else?—food. We spend fifteen seconds on the blessing and the rest of the day eating.

But far too often, we don't use food enough to soothe our emotional needs. And that is a true shame. In a recent double blind clinical study at the Joy Behar School of Dramatic Arts in Elmira, New York, it was proven that one Krispy Kreme cream-filled glazed doughnut (double-dipped in chocolate) was five times better than Prozac to reduce the symptoms of depression long term.

At John Gorrie Elementary School in Elmhurst, Massachusetts, half the kids in grades one through four were given the popular drug Ritalin, while the other half were provided an all-sugar diet, beginning with Twinkies first thing in the morning. The Twinkie kids out-performed the other kids academically three to one and were better behaved to boot. It is proven: There is nothing like sugar to calm your child.

"It's best if you get your kids started on sugar at birth," says Dr. Cynthia Magera of the University Center For Nursing Women in Oak Hills, Idaho. "Our studies have found that the children of women who dip their nipples in a simple sugar solution before breastfeeding were less prone to the typical childhood diseases."

While they discovered that nothing soothes a baby like a sugar-dipped nipple, there were downsides, for the children were more apt to breastfeed straight through to adolescence. But wouldn't you love to be guaranteed a healthy child? There are always trade-offs.

Change Is Tough, But Following Our Program Is Not

Getting started is always the most challenging part of anything, especially if you are not used to constant gorging. If you are thin, no matter how gourmet the food, because you haven't been accustomed to eating mass quantities, you'll need to plan and focus. We have developed ways to make it easier, and this book walks you through the process. Use this book in combination with the *Fast Food Restaurant Association Handbook on Good Eats,* and you'll be on your way to a whole new world in no time.

Get a Little Help from a Friend

An extremely important part of our program is support and accountability. We strongly encourage you to find three other people who need to gain weight. Choose those who face much the same challenges you do. For example, if you want to gain sixty pounds, don't pick someone who only wants to gain ten. And select someone who is equally motivated. It is much more fun to follow this program with a team of like-minded people, so make this your first priority. If you can't find someone like-minded, choose any overweight person; some accountability is better than none.

If you are having trouble finding that special person, I have found that Dunkin' Donuts and buffet restaurants are super places to locate the support you need. If nothing else works, just stand outside a local KFC, and I guarantee you'll find someone faster than a fly can lick the icing off a day-old Pepperidge Farm Butter Cake. Although, you should never have a day-old anything. In my house, the only true sin is to let the sun rise on anything with sugar.

Family, friends, and coworkers can and should play an integral and supportive role toward your success with our Seven-Day Quick-Gorge and Robust Gourmet programs. You'd be surprised at how many people say that they'll support their family member or friend, but really never do—and end up sabotaging their efforts by bringing steamed veggies and organic soy milk into the home.

Please have the people you live and associate with daily read this entire book, especially the section entitled Giving Support: Do You Know What It's About? I hope that it will provide them with some perspective on how to be supportive.

Stressed Spelled Backwards: Desserts

We all get stressed. When does stress affect you most? In the morning after getting your kids off to school? During rush hour traffic? On vacation? After or during a business meeting? Mid-afternoon or mid-morning? Dealing with a particular client or friend? Dealing with Mom? Taking care of sick kids or parents? You decide what makes you stressed, and prepare to take care of yourself in advance.

There is always a bag of mini powdered sugar doughnuts in my car and Raspberry Godiva Chocolate Truffles in my office for those stressful times. You never want to be caught off guard. Why go through even momentary anguish when it takes only a second to stuff a mini doughnut in your mouth?

What do you reach for when you are stressed? Too often people go for carrots, apples, celery, or all of these. Think about your most stressful times, and make quality substitutions for your typical food outlets. Instead of garlic pickles, try munching on a bag of Garlic Lay's Potato Chips. Instead of a piece of fruit, try bagels dipped in Nutella. If you are prone to stress, being on this program will help reduce your level of stress considerably.

Above all, never use exercise to counter stress. Substituting an activity other than food—such as yoga, swimming, jogging, weight lifting, or walking—during stressful situations will only take a negative toll on you. So we encourage you to eat something sweet or with a high fat content, which will allow you to combat stressful situations on a more even keel.

In the March issue of the *Journal of Anal-Retentive Stress Disorder Research*, internationally well-known stress creator, Dr. Blackshear Thornton Hartley, Jr., who holds several chairs at the prestigious Andrew College Institute of Visiting Fellows in Cuthbert, Georgia, put it this way: "Too much stress is not good for you."

For many of us, boredom is a major source of stress. So kick back in your La-Z-Boy recliner and watch TV. Nothing keeps your mind busier than an hour of Jerry Springer. Live a purpose-driven life.

Analyze the People around You

Analyze fat people. You heard us right. For one entire week, start looking at fat people—people who are twenty pounds or more overweight. Watch how they eat. Watch what they eat. Look at how they sit in a chair, how they get out of a chair, how they fold their arms, how they cross their legs. Notice how they just sit while their kids play. Take this seriously. Study them. You just may see yourself one day if you look hard enough. Ask yourself, "Do I really want to continue down my current path of eating light?" Now answer the question, "What would someone see if they followed me?"

Okay, for a week, you've been looking at fat people. Now, start looking at thin people. Notice what they eat, how they sit, how they carry themselves, what they wear, how they play. What differences do you see between the people with girth and the scrawny little people you are watching this week? Which do you want to be most like? That's an easy question, isn't it?

Salad and exercise are part of the daily lives of the skinny. I bet they would give up their sesame tofu and sprouts to take your place on the couch any day of the week.

Reach Out and Touch a Nice Soft Body

We've really gone too far now. But you heard us right. Find a trusting overweight soul, and reach out and touch his or her soft body. Be careful here—we don't mean strangers. But we're serious: Touch a soft tricep, calf, stomach, thigh. Feel how good soft feels. Compare a toned hard tricep to a soft flabby underarm. There is no comparison. Wouldn't you rather wake up next to a soft fleshy belly?

Trigger Foods

What triggers your desire for more food? Find those foods and keep them ready on hand. What do you reach for when you are stressed or out of control? Nuts, potato chips, chocolate, bread, pizza? Good! Don't avoid these foods—just the opposite! Find ways to *increase* their calorie content. For example: Never eat a chip without dip, try chocolate dipped in chocolate, and pour extra-virgin olive oil and sprinkle more Parmesan cheese on each slice of pizza. These little tricks will make all the difference as you find your way to a whole new and bigger you.

We are encouraging you to get in touch with the emotions associated with your trigger foods. If something just sends you over the edge, don't avoid it, eat through it. Don't fight it—let the trigger food take mastery over you. You've got to change your mentality for the long haul. You should never feel deprived on our program. Deprivation enhances desire, so if you desire something—always give in and go for it!

Night Eating . . . There Is No Better Time to Eat

With a hectic schedule, little league games, and family responsibilities, it is sometimes impossible to think about dinner before 9:00 P.M. That's good. The later you eat, the better it is for solid weight gain. This next week, have your last meal no earlier than 7:00 P.M. and your last snack fifteen minutes before bedtime. Even though we want you to eat a good breakfast, night eating is absolutely the best time to eat for fast weight gain. Television should help you relax enough to enjoy a good snack every fifteen minutes or so. Some encourage taking a twenty-minute stroll after dinner—please don't. Instead, pop in one of your virtual exercise CDs, and relax to the oldies.

A Word about Fat

With all these no-fat foods in stores these days, you'd think that fat was bad for you. Actually our bodies need fat. We believe the best fat to fry with is lard, and the best fat to cook with is butter. Butter is dairy—and remember that dairy is good for your bones! Nobelly Prize winner Dr. Brittany Lane Bailey of Smithfield University, in Oconomowoc, Wisconsin, writes: "Our research clearly shows that eating a pound of butter a day will strengthen bones to where one will never have to worry about a bone fracture when reaching 100 years of age and beyond." What more evidence do you need? If you can add sugar to your fat intake, all the better. Actually, we want you to increase the amount of the fat you consume by at least 20 percent per week.

When to Eat

Our moms used to say, "Eat like a king at breakfast, a queen at lunch, and a pauper at dinner." Actually, if anything, you should reverse this process and enjoy your heaviest food in the late evenings. But the best approach is to consume mass quantities of food a minimum of six times a day, beginning with a huge carbohydrate-infused breakfast. Never, ever walk around hungry!

Group Eating: Get Your Friends Involved

Group eating is a great way to increase pounds in a short time. And it's fun too. Begin today by inviting your friends over to help you prepare meals for your families. Casseroles are so much fun to prepare with friends: There is no bonding experience better than opening cans of thick mushroom soup to add to your special recipe.

Peeling potatoes, stirring the mac and cheese, and spreading the icing on the cake are all great ways to keep your friends involved with your new program. And it can help them too! Friends helping friends. Isn't that what it's all about?

Excuses, Excuses, Excuses

What's your excuse for remaining fit and trim? We've heard so many excuses for not adopting a weighty lifestyle: "I'm too busy to eat all day, too caught up with the kids, too depressed, dealing with my divorce, going on vacation, I love exercise." What's your excuse? Be honest with yourself. You're thin. You don't eat enough. For 99.9 percent of people, it's *not* a thyroid problem.

Insanity = doing the same thing over and over, expecting different results

The fact is that you're in a rut. Light eating and exercise has become a habit for you, an addiction. You've purchased this program for a reason: to break the cycle of poor eating habits. Your first assignment is to not offer any excuses. If you go off the plan for a moment by eating fruits and vegetables, grab a Milky Way and get right back on track. Just put an end to the excuses and move on.

Clear the Clutter

Immediately clear the clutter from your home, car, and office. Believe it or not, many studies show that clutter keeps us from focusing on a project and doing it well. At this time in your life, there is no bigger project than your desire to change your eating patterns and to gain weight. So do the spring-cleaning now! Clear the clutter, get focused, and make it happen.

Meditation

Meditation and positive thinking are key to most successful change. So when you feel overwhelmed, frustrated, hopeless, and lacking in appetite, go to a quiet place and meditate, think positive thoughts, and visualize your success. Seek relief from the daily stresses of life. Take up yoga (just *not* the vigorous type that burns lots of calories) or, better yet, learn stress relaxation. It will help you reach your goals.

Giving Support: Do You Know What It's About?

For Family and Friends

Okay, you've seen your spouse, parent, friend, or coworker start and stop this program over and over again for years. It all begins the same way: the person you know is all excited and pumped, maybe spending hundreds of dollars on some new fad, pills, shots, program after program, pre-packaged fast food, you name it, because he or she has tried everything to gain weight, to no avail. You've seen this person begin with abundant enthusiasm—declaring emphatically "This is the time!"—and then end it all by going back to exercise, sometimes within hours of starting a new weight gain program.

It's okay; just stick with them.

To be successful with this program, this person needs your total support. Complete support. Wholehearted support. You need to ask yourself the following questions, and discuss your answers:

- Will I give my support for this endeavor? If so, how? If not, why not?
- Will I ask her to tell me exactly how she would like me to support her?
- Will I listen and repeat back what I hear?
- Can I help him hold himself accountable?
- Can I give my support for the duration?

Here are some concrete suggestions that will help you provide support:

- When you eat with him, always encourage him to eat a great deal of food, and maybe a little extra. If it's at a restaurant, be an active partner in selecting buffets and pancake houses. If eating at home, encourage eating high-fat, high-sugar foods with abundant portions—no more small plates of grilled chicken and steamed broccoli.
- If you are thin, and you like to eat steamed or baked anything, don't do so around this person—it isn't fair. Why offer temptation?
- And if you are too thin—join this program as well. You both need encouragement, structure, and accountability. Provide it for each other.
- Offer to virtual exercise with this person; it's more fun to do it together. Plan outings to a grocery or food court daily.
- When there are special events, parties, or vacations, don't say, "You can go off it just this one time." Encourage him to eat as much as possible . . . and often.
- Understand that she will not always feel like eating. Maybe she's full from the day before; this doesn't mean she is off the program. Depending on the amount of weight to gain, this can be a long process. After the initial fifteen- to twenty-five-pound gain on our Seven-Day Quick-Gorge program, a good weight gain is between five to seven pounds per week. More than that is considered unhealthy. However, a one-pound-a-week weight gain is okay—who wouldn't be pleased with gaining fifty-two pounds in a single year? This is a journey to a new way of life. Understand that some weeks she may not gain any weight, usually because she hasn't been focusing on the program. Get into her emotions. Care for her. Ask her how you can help and encourage her to get back to eating with gusto.

- If you see this person deviate from the program, don't shy away from asking about it. Ask what you can do to help. Keep in mind that there is a difference between being supportive and being a nag. Learn the difference. Ask how you can be supportive when (not if) he wanders off course.
- Get in touch with your own fears. Do you really want this person to gain weight? Be honest with your feelings and emotions. It's okay to have these feelings. But it is not okay to sabotage your mate or friend because of your fears or your fast metabolism and inability to increase your weight.
- Help her feel safe. She may be embarrassed to tell you how little she weighs, the pitifully small amounts she ate that day, or that she skipped her morning snacks. Let her know that she can tell you anything.

If you share the same household:

- Stock the cabinets and the fridge with huge amounts of high-fat, high-sugar, high-calorie foods. Doughnuts and ice cream are always good bets.
- Remember too that it's not fair to have her cook one meal for herself and bake, broil, and steam a meal for you. Get used to eating fried everything. Regardless of how you are built, eating fried is fine for you too. So get with the program!

The bottom line is to be supportive. Ask what being supportive means to this person, then take those steps if you can. If you can't, make it clear. Maybe you can reach some common ground. Communication is the key in all relationships, from marriage to friendships and parent/child relationships. You can't beat a healthy open conversation with someone you care about.

Chapter Two

THE SMART START: OUR SEVEN-DAY QUICK-GORGE PROGRAM

Rise and shine, Sunshine. This is the beginning of a new day. Run over to that mirror of yours and give yourself a great big smile, then a great big bear hug. Even if you don't feel like it, fake it: It will become real soon enough. Imagine yourself the way you want to look: a hefty 300 pounds, or even more. Ralph Waldo Emerson wrote, "Nothing happens unless first a dream."

It's time to make your dreams reality. Don't let the depression of being thin control you another nanosecond. Focus on today, and only today and assure yourself that you are worth more than any steamed vegetable or raw fruit. Below are suggestions for breakfast, lunch, dinner, and a couple of snacks in between.

One solid piece of advice: *Don't skip any meals!* Success is in your control.

The Faster You Eat, the Better

At the Utah Clinic for the Morbidly Thin, thirty miles outside Scottsdale, Arizona, head research scientist Dr. Daniel Castro found that the morbidly thin were witnessed repeatedly chewing every bite of their food at least twenty-five times, producing excessively slow eating habits. Their hefty successful counterparts, however, were more apt to quickly gobble the food put before them.

The conclusion after years of research on literally thousands of thins was that the people who eat slowly are less apt to increase body weight. So if you want to gain weight, and we assume that that's why you bought this book, eat every meal as if it was your last. The faster, the better.

Beginning Your Day

It is critical to your overall weight gain program to begin each and every morning with the right amount of sugars and fats. Above all, eat quickly in the morning—and throughout the day, enjoying every last mouthful.

A Sample Day on the North Beach Diet

Pre-Breakfast Wake-Up

- 1 (16-ounce) glass of ice cold root beer mixed with 2 scoops of Häagen-Dazs vanilla ice cream.
- Sit down or recline in a La-Z-Boy Recliner for thirty minutes of newspaper reading or television watching.
- Stretch and resistance training (three days this week—see below).

Note: You will note that we provide suggested amounts this initial week, because we do not want you to fall below a certain food level for optimum weight gain. If, however, you can eat more—please, by all means, do so, for we never want you to either wake up or go to bed hungry, especially during your first week.

Breakfast

We highly recommend that you never skip a meal on the North Beach Diet plan; if, however, you are going to omit any meal, let breakfast be the only one.

- 1 (16-ounce) glass of ice cold freshly squeezed orange juice
- 6 buttermilk pancakes covered in butter and maple syrup
- 1 pound Jimmy Dean sausage (mild or hot)
- ½ pound Oscar Mayer fried bologna
- 3 eggs (fried or scrambled—cooked with bacon grease)
- 2 cups grits (if you are from the south) or 2 cups hash brown

potatoes (if you are from the north)—our preference is that you consume both, and with at least ¼ pound of butter
- 2 toasted bagels with cream cheese and strawberry preserves
- ⅓ cup Big Valley Mixed Berries (thawed) or ⅓ cup cantaloupe (when in season)
- 1 (8-ounce) glass of ice cold water
- Coffee with heavy cream and sugar

Mid-Morning Snack

- 1 can sugar cola
- 4 Krispy Kreme hot glazed doughnuts
- 1 king-size candy bar for extra energy

Lunch At Wendy's

- 1 giant Big Gulp 72-ounce soft drink (picked up at 7-11 on the way to Wendy's)
- 1 Wendy's fried chicken sandwich with extra cheese and mayo
- 1 large order of french fries
- 1 baked potato with butter and sour cream
- 1 large chili to pour over baked potato
- 1 large Frosty

Mid-Afternoon Snack

- 2 cans Dr. Pepper or other favorite drink
- 1 pound bag cheesy cheese puffs
- 1 bag Pepperidge Farm milk chocolate Milano cookies

Important Note: Doughnuts Aren't Just for Breakfast Anymore.

Dinner

- 1 pound fried round steak
- 2 fried pork chops
- 1 pound mashed red-skin potatoes with oven-roasted garlic, blue cheese, butter, and cream

- 4 cups canned creamed corn
- 3 cups Rice-a-Roni
- 8 slices Texas cheese toast
- A few slices of our homemade cheesecake with berry compote and whipped cream (each day choose a dessert from our list of options)

After-Dinner Mid-Evening Snack

- 1 bag Paul Newman's microwave butter flavor popcorn: Melt a half stick of real butter, pour over top of bag and shake (the bag, not yourself)
- Keep a liter of ice cold cola by your side throughout the evening—it is important that you do not get dehydrated
- 7-Up and vanilla ice cream float
- 1 chocolate brownie

Minutes before Bedtime

We strongly urge you to rummage through your fridge to see what you might nosh on before bedtime. Maybe a ham sandwich and a slice of that leftover apple pie, maybe some chips and dip. Bring the food to bed with you, sit at the edge, finish the last bite, say your prayers, turn out the light, and know that you've been successful another day. One day at a time . . . that's all we ask. Congratulations! You've met your goal. If you feel like congratulating yourself again—go make yourself a root beer float.

WARNING!
If You've Found That You've Burned Too Many Calories In A Given Day—Consume Four Double Stuff Oreo Cookies For Every 200 Calories Burned

---

queer eye
FOR THE THIN · GUY

The Marscapone Makeover

After a frantic plea to plump up her skinny fiancée, the *FAB 5* feeds a thin Italian immigrant from the Bronx massive amounts of tiramisu for an unforgettable hour in a live pre-recorded broadcast you and your family will be talking about for years to come.

"...family entertainment at its finest."
—JERRY FALWELL, LIBERTY NETWORK

BRAVO
Tuesdays
10:00 P.M. Eastern, 9:00 P.M. Central

PARENTS BEWARE: INTERNET DANGER FOR CHILDREN

The internet is loaded with traps to lure unsuspecting children into their webs. It is critical to be aware of problem websites your kids may link to. We recommend keeping the computer in, or near, the kitchen so you will be able to monitor what your child is viewing on the net.

The websites we are most concerned with, which should be blocked at all costs, are:

- www.weightwatchers.com
- www.slimfast.com
- www.jennycraig.com
- www.richardsimmons.com
- www.overeatersanonymous.org
- www.drphil.com
- www.americanheartassociation.com

Note On The Dr. Atkins Weight Loss Program: We were planning to list the Atkins website as dangerous to kids, but after extensive review of their plan, *except for the noncarbs*, it meets with our guarded approval.

Chapter Three

THE SLOW START:
LET YOUR FORK POINT NORTH

While we encourage you to eat massive amounts from the moment you wake up to the moment your head hits the pillow, some just want to put on a few pounds. This program is for those slow starters.

Breakfast
- ½ grapefruit
- 1 slice whole wheat toast
- 8 ounces skim milk

Lunch
- 4 ounces lean broiled chicken breast
- 1 cup steamed zucchini
- 1 Oreo cookie

Mid-Afternoon Snack
- The rest of the package of Oreos
- 2 pints rocky road ice cream, nuts, cherries, and whipped cream
- 1 jar hot fudge sauce

Dinner
- 2 loaves garlic bread
- 2 large pepperoni and mushroom pizzas (extra cheese)
- 2 large pitchers of Coke
- 3 Milky Way candy bars

Late Evening Snack

- Entire Sara Lee cheesecake—eaten directly from the freezer
- Eat every two hours from this point until bedtime

Sound Diet Tips

- Eat proud! When eating in public, choose the highest calorie foods available in the marketplace. It is our responsibility to be a role model for the light eater. And above all—never let a thin person see you consume fruits or vegetables . . . it sends the wrong message.
- Sodas and candy bars are essential to the North Beach Diet experience—never leave home without them.
- Hot chocolate, brandy, toast, warm chocolate cake, and all Pepperidge Farm products are considered medicinal, thus should be taken with other foods.
- Avoid being seen with thin people. While it is true that you will probably look bigger if you hang around with smaller people, they are actually a bad influence.
- Going to the movies at least three times a week is an essential component to lasting success on our program. Before taking your seat(s), you must purchase two extra large non–diet sodas, two boxes of Milk Duds, one bucket of popcorn with lots of butter,★ nachos with cheese, Junior Mints, and red licorice.

  ★Most theaters have self-serve butter, ask the counter staff to provide you with an extra cup, fill with their delicious mock-butter, and continuously pour over popcorn. If there is any left over, drink it along with your Milk Duds—oh so good!!!

Dining Out

Dining out should never be a problem while on the North Beach Diet. Simple planning before you begin is key to your overall success with this program. On day one, the first thing we want you to do is secure the menus from the top ten restaurants you frequent.

If there are no fast food restaurants on the list, you may very well want to re-evaluate your commitment to our plan. Are you really going to take this seriously and follow through? If at least 30 percent of your choices are not fast food restaurants, we suggest you wait a week to determine if your commitment is real.

Once you have acquired the menus, sit at the dining room table with your entire family and determine what foods are best to achieve your overall goal. First and foremost, many restaurants are very helpful in this regard by putting little red heart symbols next to the menu items we don't recommend. Cross those off your food choices immediately.

Some restaurants are helpful by listing the amount for calories, fat grams, and the sodium content for each menu item. This is particularly beneficial in your quest to remain on the fat-track program. With a black marker, we suggest you immediately cross off all foods with a heart symbol or in the "low-cal" category. Black them out completely so you are not the least bit tempted. Often it's difficult to make the right choices while sitting in the restaurant, so plan ahead.

Some quick hints to following our program while dining out:

- Begin eating bread and butter from the first moment you arrive. Ask for more when you've emptied the bread basket.
- We suggest no salad; however, if you must have a salad, order two (or more) extra dressings with a side of crumbled blue cheese. Thousand island, ranch, and blue cheese are our suggested options, again with a side of crumbled blue cheese.
- Chicken and seafood should be fried—never baked, broiled, or steamed. Note: If the establishment does not offer fried foods, leave immediately.
- Steaks should be topped with herbed butter and served with rich sauces such as béarnaise or hollandaise. Please, never use ketchup on a fine steak.
- There should be only two choices for potatoes: fried or loaded with cheese, butter, sour cream, and bacon. Ask for your french fries to be tossed in garlic butter—all fine restaurants should accommodate.
- Desserts should always be served à la mode. If no ice cream is served, excuse yourself, find a convenient store, and buy a quart of the ice cream that will go best with the dessert you plan to order. Most fine restaurants will allow you to bring in what they do not serve.
- Salt your food generously before tasting. Salt is good for you. Never, ever use lemon juice, Mrs. Dash, or Spike as sodium substitutes. If you have hypertension, pop a blood pressure pill and salt away. Furthermore, if you have high blood pressure, don't blame the salt, blame your doctor for not providing the proper medication . . . drugs are just too plentiful for you not to be on one.

Spend a Relaxing Week Down on Our NON-ORGANIC Idaho Potato Fat Farm

ENJOY THE GORGEOUS FARM LAND OF WHEELING, WEST VIRGINIA, AND THE GREAT OUTDOORS LIKE YOU'VE NEVER IMAGINED WHILE COMMUNING WITH NATURE ON OUR LUXURIOUS 157-ACRE NON-ORGANIC FAT FARM. AS A SPECIAL TREAT, EACH GUEST IS ASSIGNED FOUR THIN FIELD HANDS, CATERING TO YOUR EVERY NEED AND WHIM.

DAY ONE Park your butt in a plush hammock while drinking mint juleps and munching on Mississippi mud pie, as you watch your thin field hands pick fresh corn and potatoes for all your evening meals.

DAY TWO From the viewpoint of a mountaintop, relax in a lavish La-Z-Boy recliner while noshing on fried buffalo wings and sipping on double-rich chocolate cream shakes. You'll thoroughly enjoy watching your thin field hands harvest wheat, removing all the natural nutrients, and processing it into fine white flour for the making of the most delicious homemade white bread you'll ever taste. Served at all meals and snacks with plenty of butter.

DAY THREE AND BEYOND No more lying down on the farm: Your experience will be hands-on from this point forward. From the vantage point of your super-padded GPS-equipped golf cart, you'll ride around the fields directing your personal farm hands as you see fit. If you want corn one night—order it picked. Potatoes? They are at your beck and call—and everything is fresh picked on your orders.

Leave the Kids At Home
Learn How to Work a Down-Home Farm Without Lifting a Finger

OUR FARM GUARANTEE
"Gain 13½ pounds in just one week, or Your Money Back."
— KATHERINE AND SCOTT EIBEL, PROPRIETORS

IDAHO POTATO FAT FARMS, INC.

For Costs & Details Visit:
www.northbeachdietonline.com
Diner's Club Card Only

PART II
ROBUST GOURMET

Chapter Four

GAINING WEIGHT HAS NEVER TASTED SO GOOD

Food is "the" essential ingredient to a happy and productive life. Nothing beats eating abundant quantities of good food to satisfy your every need.

In this section, we are providing some of our favorite and tastiest recipes to help you achieve maximum weight gain on our program.

The most important component about our plan is never to skip a meal or snack. You *must* eat a minimum of six times a day; and always be on the lookout for ways to increase your intake of fat, refined sugars, and white flour. We realize, however, that life is fast paced and hectic and that there will be times when you'll miss a meal—so just double up the next time you eat.

Remember, you are on a path of enlightenment to a whole new you—a journey that will help let the real you break through!

Desserts, Glorious Desserts

Most cookbooks and recipe sections end with dessert recipes—we humbly disagree with this, so we begin with our fabulous desserts. If you are rushed and have no time for a complete meal, we strongly urge you to grab something sweet.

Before and After Meals

If possible, and it should be, eat dessert both before and after each meal: Studies confirm that sugar assists in the digestive process. Dr. Andria Rogers, of the prestigious Borgeson Institute for the Celebrity Thin, wrote about her research: "If you sandwich a meal between desserts, 83.4 percent of those tested were less apt to suffer from heartburn, acid reflux, or any other type of digestive disorder."

Sundays are great days to make all your desserts for the entire week. Freeze and store them for the week.

We recommend that you consume no less than two different desserts per day—yes, compared to other diet programs this may seem a bit excessive; but you are on the fat-track program now, and success is within your grasp.

Just Add Cocoa

As we previously stated, sugar, butter, and flour are essentials to overall health and happiness in life. However, research has found that by simply adding cocoa to the above three ingredients, the healing elements are unmatched in comparison to other therapeutic measures. It is proven: Nothing can nurture us back from a stressful day better than a warm piece of delicately rich chocolate cake right out of the oven.

A triple-blind study conducted at the Baton Twirling College in Winona, Mississippi, by the internationally acclaimed professor of gastronomic affairs, Dr. Rosemary Henderson, PhD, LMNOP, found that the negative effects of stress were alleviated five times more powerfully by the consumption of warm chocolate cake than by the leading brand of pharmaceutical pain medicine.

Dr. Henderson recently spoke at the prestigious conference on Food and Tantrums (FAT) held at an undisclosed food manufacturing plant in Hershey, Pennsylvania: "It's conclusive: A warm piece of chocolate cake has the essential components to heal all that ails mankind." Hence the FDA is allowing all foodstuffs containing cocoa to use the word "medicinal" on the label.

With this sound and incontrovertible truth, we begin our dessert recipe section with—what else—the best chocolate cake you'll ever taste.

MEDICINAL CHOCOLATE CAKE

Eat this! It will make you feel better.

–DR. BARBARA DOWELL

Chocolate Cake

1 stick butter

2 cups sugar

1 teaspoon vanilla extract

2 eggs

¾ cup "medicinal" Hershey's Cocoa

1¾ cups unsifted all-purpose flour

¾ teaspoon baking powder

¾ teaspoon baking soda

⅛ teaspoon salt

1¾ cups milk

Vanilla Butter Cream Icing

2 sticks salted butter (softened)

6 cups powdered sugar

2 teaspoons real vanilla

Enough whole milk to moisten icing consistency (about 6 tablespoons)

Preheat oven to 350 degrees. Generously grease and flour two 9-inch round cake pans. Cream butter, sugar, and vanilla until fluffy; blend in eggs. Combine cocoa, flour, baking powder, baking soda, and salt in bowl; add alternately with milk to batter. Blend well. Pour into prepared pans; bake for 30 to 40 minutes or until cake tester inserted in center comes out clean. Cool 10 minutes; remove from pans.

While the research remains new, initial results are showing that the medicinal benefits of this chocolate cake are greatly enhanced by icing the cake with either chocolate or vanilla butter cream icing. And it's always best served with vanilla ice cream. To make the icing, combine in bowl butter, powdered sugar, vanilla, and enough milk to make spreadable. For chocolate vanilla butter cream icing add cocoa before adding the milk.

Note: If using for healing purposes, do not frost, and eat one entire cake round before cooling takes effect.

·HELP SAVE THE TWINKIE·

FATS UNITED AGAINST THIN TYRANNY

Because of all the Low-Carb diets, Hostess, the maker of Twinkies went bankrupt. Please join our campaign.

1) The first Tuesday of each month (8:35 P.M.- in whichever time zone you live), dim your kitchen lights for 1 minute to pay homage to our dear friend.

2) Buy, and eat, 1 box of Twinkies per day.

3) Purchase additional boxes of Twinkies and hand them to those walking into organizations like Weight Watchers and Jenny Craig ... they need to hear the truth.

4) Press an individual Twinkie cellophane wrapper into an even flat strip, fold into a ribbon, and wear every day until this crisis is averted. Make extra for your friends and ostracize anyone who will not wear a Twinkie ribbon ... they are un-American.

One dark night in October, the North Beach Diet Gang with the Keebler Elves stole the Oscar Mayer Wienermobile, picked up Little Debbie, Sara Lee, and the Pillsbury Dough Boy. They were going to kidnap Dr. Atkins and force-feed him Twinkies until he caved in and stopped advocating a no-carb diet. However, they found that he unfortunately had already died ... it's said that he died from a fall, but we believe it was from not eating carbs. Beware—the North Beach Diet gang is on the lookout.

BATTERED FRIED TWINKIES

What better way to express your love for someone than a Battered Fried Twinkie? There is none. However, sadness befalls us as we offer this recipe, as we have learned that Hostess, the maker of Twinkies, filed for bankruptcy protection in September 2004. It seems as though too many people are following the no-carb craze.

The "thins" are trying to press their wrong-headed, left-wing agenda on the rest of us. We cannot let this happen! We recommend that all North Beach Dieters try this recipe and share it with their friends.

Batter

        1 cup all-purpose flour
        1 tablespoon malt vinegar
        1 teaspoon baking powder
        1 teaspoon salt
    1½ cups water
        1 box fresh Twinkies

Raspberry Couli

        1 package frozen raspberries, thawed, or 1 pint fresh raspberries
        1 cup sugar
    ¼ cup Grand Marnier (orange liqueur)

In a skillet heat 3 inches of oil over medium-high heat. Combine flour, malt vinegar, baking powder, and salt. Slowly stir in water until a custard-like consistency develops. Roll the Twinkie in batter and fry in hot oil for about 90 seconds, or until golden brown.

Make the raspberry couli by blending raspberries, sugar, and orange liqueur. Put 3 tablespoons of raspberry couli on a chilled dessert plate, place fried Twinkie on top of couli, and add two scoops of vanilla ice cream, another drizzle of couli, and a dollop of whipped cream.

BEER-BATTERED DEEP-FRIED SNICKERS

Milky Ways are another good candy bar for frying. We encourage you to experiment with any type of candy you can think of—and let us know which one tastes best to you.

1 dozen Snickers Bars
Oil for deep frying

Batter

2 bottles Heineken beer
1 cup all-purpose flour
½ cup corn flour
⅛ teaspoon baking soda

2 packages Jell-O Instant Butterscotch Pudding
Redi-Whip
¼ cup crushed roasted peanuts
6 Maraschino cherries (with stem)

Drink one beer before starting. Chill the Snickers Bars for at least 2 hours in the refrigerator—not the freezer. Heat 3 inches oil in skillet over medium-high heat. Mix flours and baking soda and add the second bottle of Heineken beer to make a consistency of cream. Dip the chilled Snickers in batter, and fry until golden brown.

Make two batches of Jell-O Instant Butterscotch Pudding. Place ½ cup of prepared pudding on a chilled plate, and top with two Beer-Battered Deep-Fried Snickers Bars. Spray a generous amount of Redi-Whip and top with crushed roasted peanuts and a Maraschino cherry.

Makes 6 servings

HE WAS ONLY A CHOCOLATE CHIP COOKIE BUT I LOVED HIM

I met him at a party. There he was at the end of the buffet, a loner, the last one on the plate. He had a certain something, a sweetness, a sensuality. He was one hot cookie.

I felt as if I'd always known him, always hungered for him. When he looked at me with those warm brown eyes, I melted. Before I knew it, I had my hands on him, my mouth on him, in public. After that night, we were inseparable.

With him, I could be myself. He didn't seem to care what mood I was in, how I looked, even if I gained weight. Together, we had the recipe for happiness. No one satisfied me like Chip! Then things changed. My friends said he wasn't good enough for me. I now only wanted him with ice cream. I felt crummy. I knew the end was near.

Now we've gone our separate ways. I hardly think of him anymore. Oh, if I see a certain TV commercial, a particular magazine ad, a coupon for ten cents off, that old longing returns. And when we run into each other in the supermarket, we nod. We're friendly. But it's over. I'm now looking for Mr. Goodbar.

—Anonymous

THE MARK MERRILL SWEET POTATO PIE

This recipe won first place in the 1992 Mark Merrill Sweet Potato Pie Invitational, held each year on February 30 in Eufaula, Alabama, commemorating the untimely passing of Mr. Merrill in 1984, from a sweet potato purposely infected with botulism by the second place winner.

    3 pounds sweet potatoes, peeled and boiled until tender
    1 stick salted butter (softened)
    3 eggs
    1 can evaporated milk
 1¼ cups granulated sugar
 1¼ cups light brown sugar
    2 teaspoons ground nutmeg
    1 teaspoon vanilla extract
  ½ teaspoon ground cinnamon (plus a little to sprinkle on top of
    pie before baking)
  ½ teaspoon salt
    Pie shell (homemade or Pillsbury refrigerated pie shell)

Allow sweet potatoes to cool and place in electric mixer. Add butter and eggs and beat until light. Add milk, sugars, nutmeg, vanilla, cinnamon, and salt and beat until combined. Preheat oven to 450 degrees. Pour mixture into unbaked pie shell(s). Place on the bottom rack of oven for 15 minutes. Then place on middle rack and bake another 30 to 45 minutes at 350 degrees, or until a knife inserted into the middle of pie comes out clean. Let cool, but never refrigerate. Best eaten at room temperature.

Makes 2 (8 to 9-inch) pies or 1 (10-inch) pie

MCDONALD'S HOT APPLE PIE À LA MODE

What could be more American than apple pie from McDonald's? While this treat is not homemade, it is special and tastes really good, too!

4 McDonald's hot apple pies (yes, we realize they are baked, not fried, but they are still tasty)

2 pints Häagen-Dazs vanilla cinnamon swirl ice cream

1 package mini M&Ms (optional)

½ cup Smucker's caramel sauce

1 container Cool Whip or homemade whipped cream

½ cup Marshmallow Fluff

¼ cup crushed toasted pecans

4 Maraschino cherries (with stem)

Take McDonald's hot apple pie and scoop ice cream on top. Add M&Ms, caramel sauce, whipped cream, Marshmallow Fluff, pecans, and a cherry on top. Repeat with the remaining pies.

Makes 1 or 2 servings

WENDY'S CHOCOLATE FROSTY SMASH

1 large Wendy's Frosty (we suggest buying 2, freezing the extra one
  and serving it at breakfast instead of juice)
8 crushed Nutter Butter peanut butter cookies
8 crushed Oreo cookies
  Redi-Whip whipped topping
1 Maraschino cherry (with stem)

Spoon Wendy's Frosty into large bowl. Place both sets of cookies in a plastic baggie and crush with a heavy object. Add to Frosty. Spoon into 7-11 Big Gulp plastic cup. Top with Redi-Whip and cherry. We highly recommend using Nabisco Sugar Wafers as spoons; you will need two packages.

Makes 1 serving

HELPFUL HINTS FOR BAKING THE PERFECT COOKIE

- Always use a light-colored aluminum cookie sheet. Dark cookie sheets have a tendency to burn your cookies.
- Always line your cookie sheet with parchment paper. You will never have to grease or wash your pans, which makes de-panning a cinch.
- Place your cookie dough in the refrigerator for one hour before forming cookies.
- Cookies can be formed and frozen and can be baked from frozen as well.
- For a hard biscotti-type cookie, after the cookie has cooled, re-bake in a 250-degree oven for fifteen to thirty minutes. These are perfect for dunking in coffee or milk.

MOM'S MIDNIGHT SNACK SUGAR COOKIES

Of course we all love homemade cookies. Chocolate chip and oatmeal raisin are two of my favorites. The recipe on the Toll House Chocolate Chip package is the best we've found for the standard chocolate chip cookie, and the oatmeal raisin cookie recipe on the container of Quaker Oatmeal makes an excellent cookie as well. Because you can easily find those, we won't list them here.

When we were little kids, my mom used to make these wonderful sugar cookies for us to eat just before we went to bed.

    1 cup salted butter, room temperature
    2 cups granulated sugar
    2 eggs
    2 tablespoons heavy cream
    1 teaspoon vanilla extract
    ½ teaspoon salt
    2 teaspoons baking powder
    3 cups all-purpose flour

Preheat oven to 375 degrees. In electric mixer combine butter and sugar and beat well. Add eggs one at a time, and beat until fluffy. Pour into mixing bowl and mix in the remaining ingredients until well blended. Make balls out of dough and sprinkle tops of each cookie with regular granulated sugar, colored sugar crystals (for the holidays), or clear sugar crystals. Bake about 8 minutes, depending on the size of your cookie. Once baked, liberally dust with regular granulated sugar.

Makes 6 servings

Note: We suggest using an ice cream scoop to mold all cookies. Sometimes I like extra large cookies, and sometimes I like bite-size cookies. Choose the size ice cream scoop you desire and form cookies so they all come out the same size. If you don't have an ice cream scoop, use a teaspoon or tablespoon and roll into a ball.

THE FAUX NEIMAN-MARCUS COOKIE

This recipe has some folklore behind it. Many years ago (even before the Internet) it was circulated with the story about a woman getting even with Neiman-Marcus for charging her store credit card $250 for the recipe, not for cookies, only the recipe. It became such a myth that Neiman-Marcus had to debunk it in their most recent cookbook, which by the way, doesn't even include this recipe. This is such a great cookie that we're printing the recipe here. Be forewarned, it makes over ten dozen cookies. So some rainy day when you have the time, bake, eat, and enjoy!

    5 cups blended oatmeal
    2 cups butter
    2 cups granulated sugar
    2 cups brown sugar
    4 eggs
    2 teaspoons vanilla extract
    4 cups all-purpose flour
    1 teaspoon salt
    2 teaspoons baking powder
    2 teaspoons baking soda
   24 ounces chocolate chips
    1 (8-ounce) Hershey's chocolate bar, grated
    3 cups chopped pecans

Preheat oven to 375 degrees. Put oatmeal in blender or food processor and process until it becomes a fine powder. Cream butter and both sugars together. Add eggs and vanilla. In separate bowl mix together flour, oatmeal, salt, baking powder, and baking soda. Add wet ingredients to dry ingredients and mix. Stir in chocolate chips, chocolate bar, and pecans. Roll into balls (or form with an ice cream scoop), and place two inches apart on a parchment-lined, light-colored cookie sheet. Bake about 10 minutes. You may freeze extra dough.

Makes enough for 2

THE FAUX NEIMAN-MARCUS COOKIE STORY

Here is the story behind the myth, which has become an urban legend (source unknown):

My daughter and I had finished a salad at the Neiman-Marcus Café in Dallas and decided to have a small dessert. Because our family members are such "Cookie Monsters," we decided to try the Neiman-Marcus Cookie. It was so good that I asked if they would give me the recipe. She said with a frown, "I'm afraid not." Well, I said, would you let me buy the recipe? With a cute smile, she agreed. I asked how much, and she responded "Two fifty." I said with approval, "Just add it to my tab."

Thirty days later, I received my statement from Neiman-Marcus and it was $285. I looked again and remembered I had only spent $9.95 for two salads and about $20 for a scarf. As I glanced at the bottom of the statement it read "Cookie Recipe—$250.00." Boy was I upset! I called Neiman's accounting office and told them the waitress said it was two fifty, and I did not realize she meant $250 for a cookie recipe. I asked them to take back the recipe and reduce my bill, but they said they were sorry, but all the recipes were this expensive so not just anyone could duplicate the bakery recipes . . . the bill would stand.

I thought of how I could get even or try to get my money back. I just said okay, you folks got my $250 and now I'm going to have $250 worth of fun. I told her that I was going to see to it that every cookie lover will have the $250 recipe from Neiman-Marcus for nothing. She replied, "I wish you wouldn't do this." I told her that this was the only way I could get even. So here it is, please pass it on to someone else or run a few copies . . . I paid for it, now you can have it for free!

SUMPTUOUS CARROT CAKE

There are many carrot cake recipes out there—but this is our family's favorite. You must frost it with oodles and oodles of rich cream cheese frosting.

Cake

    2 cups granulated sugar
    1⅓ cups vegetable oil
    3 jumbo eggs, room temperature
    1½ teaspoons real vanilla extract
    2 cups all-purpose flour
    2 teaspoons ground cinnamon
    2 teaspoons baking soda
    1½ teaspoons salt
    3 cups grated carrots
    1 cup raisins
    1 cup chopped pecans
    1 tablespoon white all-purpose flour to mix with raisins and pecans

Frosting

    3 sticks salted butter, room temperature
    1 (8-ounce) package softened cream cheese, room temperature
    1 tablespoon real vanilla extract
    6 to 8 cups powdered sugar
    Enough whole milk to moisten to an icing consistency
    (start with 2 tablespoons)

Preheat oven to 350 degrees. Butter and flour two 9-inch or three 8-inch round cake pans. Beat sugar, oil, and eggs together with an electric mixer. Add vanilla. In separate bowl combine flour, cinnamon, baking soda, and salt. Fold dry ingredients into egg mixture, and stir until well blended. Combine grated carrots, raisins, and pecans with the white flour, and add to mixture. Bake for 30 to 40 minutes, or until a toothpick comes out clean from the center of the cake. Let cool on racks for 10 minutes, then remove from the pans.

For the frosting, place all ingredients except milk in large mixing bowl, and beat with an electric mixer until smooth, adding a tablespoon of milk at a time until the desired consistency is reached. Frost the cake and top with Bern's suggested toppings.

Makes 2 or 3 servings

Note: Extra frosting should be spread on your favorite cookie and eaten right before bedtime.

BERN'S KING MIDAS CARROT CAKE

World-renowned Bern's Steak House in Tampa, Florida, known for its aged steaks and largest (and best) restaurant wine cellar, is the place where U.S. presidents eat when they are in town. If you ever get the chance, make reservations (well in advance) for Bern's. Its incredible dessert room made from authentic wine caverns, has an extra special way of serving carrot cake. Serve each piece of carrot cake with:

2 scoops Häagen-Dazs Macadamia Brittle Crunch ice cream (of course Bern's makes its ice cream on site)

4 tablespoons (or more) Godiva Hot Fudge Sauce

1 good-size dollop of real homemade whipped cream made with sugar and vanilla

¼ cup crushed toasted macadamia nuts

1 Maraschino cherry (with stem)

LEMON MERINGUE PIE

Of all the pies in the world Lemon Meringue Pie is probably my favorite. Of course, warm apple pie with vanilla ice cream is always good. Then there's pecan and cherry. And Mississippi Mud Pie is good too. Before I go off and name every pie in the world, let me provide you with this incredible Lemon Meringue Pie recipe. You'll love every single bite.

   2 (8-inch) pie shells

Lemon Filling

   8 jumbo egg yolks
   1 cup lemon juice (fresh, never, ever bottled)
   3 cups plus 1 cup water
   1 cup cornstarch
   3 cups granulated sugar
   1 teaspoon salt
   6 tablespoons butter

Meringue

   8 egg whites
   ½ teaspoon cream of tartar
   ½ teaspoon salt
   ½ teaspoon vanilla extract
   1 cup granulated sugar

Preheat oven to 425 degrees. Line two pie pans with pie shells. Poke with fork to release air pockets while baking. Bake 8 to 15 minutes, or until shells are nicely browned. Except for the few minutes you'll be browning the meringue, you will not be baking this pie, so make sure the shell is cooked and medium brown in color. Cool completely before filling.

For lemon filling, whisk egg yolks and fresh lemon juice together in mixing bowl. Combine the 1 cup of water and cornstarch and set aside. In large saucepan, bring 3 cups of water, sugar, and salt to a boil on medium-high heat. Add cornstarch and water mixture slowly to boiling sugar water. Stir constantly with a whisk until mixture is clear and thick.

Take off stove, add egg mixture slowly, stirring constantly with a whisk. Return to stove and bring to a boil. Then remove from stove and add butter, whisking in 1 tablespoon at a time. Tightly place a piece of plastic wrap directly on lemon filling so a film will not develop on the curd. Let cool completely.

For meringue, in electric mixer, beat together egg whites, cream of tartar, salt, and vanilla until frothy. Slowly add sugar while mixer is on medium high. Beat until stiff peaks form. But be careful not to overbeat.

Reduce oven to 350 degrees. Put equal amounts of lemon curd in cooked pie shells, and pile high with meringue. Smooth with a spatula, making sure meringue touches the edges of the crust. Bake until meringue is nicely brown. Watch the pie carefully because the meringue burns easily. Cool completely, then refrigerate for at least 3 hours.

Makes 2 (8-inch) pies

THE MOST DELICIOUS BROWNIE YOU'LL EVER EAT

These brownies are a hit everywhere they are served. We have found no other brownie on earth to compare to this delicious chocolate concoction.

Brownies

2 sticks salted butter, softened

1⅔ cups granulated sugar

1 teaspoon real vanilla extract

4 jumbo eggs, room temperature

½ cup Medicinal Hershey's Cocoa

1 cup all-purpose flour

½ cup chopped pecans or walnuts (optional)

Frosting

½ cup salted butter, softened

1 cup powdered sugar

½ teaspoon vanilla extract

¼ cup Medicinal Hershey's Cocoa (more if desired)

Whole milk (enough to moisten for icing—about 1 tablespoon)

For the brownies, beat butter with electric mixer until smooth. Add sugar and beat, then add vanilla and one egg at a time, beating after each addition. Continue beating until fluffy, about 5 minutes after the last egg is added. Add Medicinal Hershey's Cocoa and beat until smooth. Add flour and beat for 30 seconds to 1 minute or until smooth. Fold in chopped pecans or walnuts if desired.

Preheat the oven to 300 degrees. Butter and flour a 9 x 13–inch baking pan. Pour in batter and bake for exactly 30 minutes. Frost when cooled.

While the brownies are cooking make the frosting. In a large bowl mix together butter, powdered sugar, vanilla, and cocoa. Add milk a little at a time while mixing until reaching desired consistency.

Makes 4 servings

Serving Suggestion: Top with Häagen-Dazs vanilla ice cream, Hershey's Chocolate Sauce, real whipped cream, toasted pecans, and a Maraschino cherry (with stem).

"SPIN THE BUCKET" WITH LITTLE DEBBIE

We realize that some days are more hectic than others, hence the need for quick, spur-of-the-moment desserts when unexpected guests drop by. You should always keep Little Debbie Snack Cakes on hand when that special moment arrives.

2 boxes Little Debbie Coffee Cakes
2 boxes Little Debbie Devil Squares
2 boxes Little Debbie Donut Sticks
2 boxes Little Debbie Blueberry Loaves
2 boxes Little Debbie Zebra Cakes
2 boxes Little Debbie Oatmeal Crème Pies
2 boxes Little Debbie Fudge Rounds
2 boxes Little Debbie Cosmic Brownies
2 boxes Little Debbie Star Crunch
2 boxes Little Debbie Strawberry Shortcakes
2 boxes Little Debbie Fudge Brownies
2 boxes Little Debbie Devil Crèmes
2 boxes Little Debbie Honey Buns
2 boxes Little Debbie Pecan Spinwheels
2 boxes Little Debbie Swiss Cake Rolls
2 boxes Little Debbie Marshmallow Supremes
2 boxes Little Debbie Nutty Bars
2 boxes Little Debbie Boston Crème Rolls
2 boxes Little Debbie Fancy Cakes

Open all boxes and place unopened individual cakes in a large bucket and stir around until completely mixed. Blindfold your guests or family members one at a time and have them reach into the "Bucket O' Cakes," securing one tasty snack cake. Have them open the package while blindfolded, and see if they can guess which tasty Little Debbie snack cake they have chosen. It's great fun!

Enough for 12 people

DOUBLE SUCKED AND FILLED JELLY DONUTS

This dessert, while nutritious and delightful, is also fun for the entire family to prepare.

2 dozen jelly filled Krispy Kreme or Dunkin Donuts doughnuts
2 quarts Häagen-Dazs ice cream (we recommend mint chocolate chip)

Together, with your family and friends (it's great fun at a party), hold one jelly doughnut with both hands with the hole placed firmly against your mouth. Suck hard until all the jelly is totally removed. Most people will have to double suck to get all the jelly out of the donut. Then with a piping bag or teaspoon, refill the donuts with soft ice cream— and enjoy.

Makes 6 servings

VIRTUAL EXPEDITIONS:

Magnificent Couch Adventures for You & The Buds

(Narrated by Blaine Bailey)

- Raft the Budweiser White Foam Rapids
- Never Leave Your Base Camp As You Follow a Sherpa Climb to the Top Of Mount Mallowmar
- Watch Killer Whales Mate Off the Coast of Newfoundland
- Hike, Canoe, Horseback Ride Miles of the Grand Canyon without Moving a Muscle

SPONSORED BY: SEDENTARY-ROOMS-TO-GO

"Reinforced Furniture for The Whole Family"

No Interest – No Payments – Ever • We Just Want You to Be Happy

THE OLN TRAIL MIX RECIPE

The Rough & Tumble Mix Propelling You to Nod Off

1 (1-pound) bag Cheetos (not Cheese Puffs)
1 (1-pound) bag mini chocolate covered pretzels
2 (12-ounce) cans fancy salted cashews
1 (15-ounce) bag Brach's chocolate covered peanuts (double coated)
1 box Fruit Loops cereal
1 (1-pound) bag plain M&Ms
1 (½-pound) bag Golden Raisins
3 bags Pepperidge Farm "Mini" Milano Cookies
1 (16-ounce) bag Frito corn chips
1 box cinnamon sugar doughnut holes

Put all the ingredients in a five-gallon bucket and mix well. Makes enough for two or three virtual expeditions.

Enhance Your OLN Expedition Experience

Fill a 3-quart *Thirst Quencher Backpack* with ice cold Budweiser, lay on the couch, sip brew (as needed), while consuming your homemade OLN trail mix.

Ahhhhhhhhhhh, now, that's outdoor life at its best!

THE FINEST CHEESECAKE YOU'LL EVER TASTE

Crust

1½ cups graham cracker crumbs

½ cup (1 stick) butter, melted

¼ cup sugar

1 teaspoon vanilla extract

6 jumbo eggs,
room temperature

Filling

4 (8-ounce) packages Philadelphia
cream cheese, room temperature

2 cups sugar

Topping

2 cups sour cream

1⅓ cups sugar

1 teaspoon vanilla extract

For crust, preheat oven to 350 degrees. Lightly butter the bottom of a 10-inch springform pan. Combine crumbs, butter, and sugar until thoroughly mixed and press into the bottom of the pan. Bake for 5 minutes. Cool.

For the filling, stir cream cheese until smooth. Add sugar and vanilla and stir again. Add eggs one at a time, beating well after each addition. Pour over the cooked crust and bake for 40 to 55 minutes. Cool for 15 minutes on a rack.

For the topping, thoroughly mix sour cream, sugar, and vanilla and pour carefully over the baked cheesecake. Bake for 10 minutes longer. Cool to room temperature and chill 12 to 24 hours before serving. Remove the side piece from pan and cut the cake into wedges.

Makes 2 to 3 servings

Serving Suggestions: Mix together 1 pint each of fresh strawberries (sliced), raspberries, and blueberries with 1 cup sugar and ½ cup Grand Marnier orange flavored liqueur. Chill for 2 hours, pour a generous portion over each slice of cheesecake, and top with a dollop of homemade whipped cream.

Variation: Buy 20 Godiva truffles in assorted flavors. After the cheesecake has baked for 10 minutes, pull from the oven and push all the truffles inside the cheesecake in random areas. Continue baking. Every single bite will be a different sensation.

APPLE CRISP

You and your guest will be smitten with this crisp. The topping is especially good with fresh mango and raspberries, served with lemon honey ice cream.

Apples

    3 Granny Smith apples
    3 McIntosh apples
    3 Golden Delicious apples
    ½ cup all-purpose flour
 1½ cups sugar
    1 tablespoon ground cinnamon
    ½ teaspoon ground nutmeg
    ½ teaspoon allspice

Topping

    ½ cup all-purpose flour
    ¾ cup brown sugar
    ⅛ teaspoon salt
    6 tablespoons salted butter
    1 cup oatmeal (quick or regular)

Peel, core, and quarter all the apples, then slice them into small pieces. Mix all the apple ingredients in a large bowl; toss until totally coated.

For the topping, place all the topping ingredients in a food processor and pulse until totally mixed, 15 to 20 pulses.

Preheat oven to 350 degrees. Place the apples in a greased 9 x 13-inch casserole pan, top with crisp topping, and bake for about 1 hour or until bubbly. Let cool for 15 minutes before serving.

Makes 2 servings

Serving Suggestions: There is only one way to eat this incredible dessert—with a generous helping of vanilla Häagen-Dazs ice cream.

WHOOPI PIES

Whoopi Pies are a New England treat. In some parts of the country they are called Globs. Your kids will love you every time you make these delicious delightful pies—and they are really easy to make.

Pie

⅓ cup vegetable oil

1 egg, lightly beaten

1 teaspoon vanilla extract

¼ teaspoon salt

1 teaspoon baking soda

1 cup sugar

⅓ cup cocoa

¾ cup milk, with 1 teaspoon vinegar added

2 cups all-purpose flour

Filling

1 stick salted butter

2 cups powdered sugar

6 tablespoons Marshmallow Fluff

½ teaspoon vanilla extract

With an electric mixer, blend oil, egg, vanilla, salt, baking soda, and sugar until smooth. Add the cocoa and milk and mix until well blended. Add the flour and mix completely, but do not overmix. Don't worry, the mixture will be somewhat runny.

It's best if you use parchment paper to line the bottom of a large cookie sheet pan. If you do not have parchment paper, you can grease the cookie sheet—but they really come out better with parchment paper, so go get some.

Preheat oven to 350 degrees. Use an ice cream scoop to ladle the batter onto the pan—about 3 tablespoons for each Whoopi Pie. They will spread, so only put about 6 to a pan—do not overcrowd. Leave about 4 inches between each pie. Bake for 8 to 12 minutes. Be careful not to overbake or underbake. Let cool completely.

While the pie is baking, make the filling. Place all the filling ingredients in a mixing bowl and beat until smooth. After the pies have cooled, spread the filling on the bottom side of pie and top with another pie. There should be none left over. If there is filling left over, you aren't following the program! You can individually wrap leftovers in clear plastic wrap.

Makes about 3 servings (5 pies per serving)

Variation: Fill them with ice cream, and make a sandwich.

HOMEMADE COUNTRY-STYLE VANILLA ICE CREAM

This is the absolute greatest homemade country-style vanilla ice cream you'll ever eat.

    3 eggs
 1¾ cups sugar
    3 cups heavy cream
    3 cups half-and-half
    2 tablespoons real vanilla extract
  ¼ teaspoon salt

In a large mixing bowl beat the eggs until foamy. Gradually add the sugar; beat until thickened and pale in color. Add the cream, half-and-half, vanilla, and salt; mix thoroughly. Chill. Churn-freeze in your ice cream maker, following its directions (I use an all-electric ice cream maker, but you can use the old-fashioned type with ice and salt as well).

Makes about 3 quarts or 1 serving

Variations: For Strawberry or Peach Ice Cream add 1 quart fresh strawberries, stemmed and chopped into very small bits or 1 quart fresh peaches, peeled and chopped into very small bits (a food processor is best for the chopping) and 2 cups sugar.

Combine the sugar and strawberries or peaches, and let sit for 3 to 4 hours. Then place in a large strainer to drain all the juice. This is a critical step because if all the juice is not drained your ice cream will have ice crystals throughout. Put fruit in the ice cream and let sit for an hour or longer before churning.

ORANGE AND CHOCOLATE CHIP COOKIE ICE CREAM

1 tablespoon orange extract (not imitation extract, the real stuff)
1 recipe vanilla ice cream (page 61)
  Red and yellow food coloring
4 to 5 cups crushed Famous Amos Chocolate Chip Cookies

Add the orange extract to the vanilla ice cream mixture and enough red and yellow food coloring—two drops of each color at a time, mixing in between—to turn it a nice rich orange color. Begin to churn the ice cream. Once it has thickened, just before your ice cream begins to labor (if you put the cookies in too soon, they will turn to mush), throw in the Famous Amos Chocolate Chip Cookies. It's critical to use hard cookies; soft ones don't work at all. Also it is critical to use a very high quality cookie with lots of chocolate chips.

You will love this ice cream!

Makes about 3½ quarts or 1 serving

"Not everyone gets to be a baker when they grow up."
–Tino Martinez

THE BEST CHOCOLATE ICE CREAM

This is by far the best chocolate ice cream you will ever taste. Of course our two favorite brands of store-bought ice cream are Häagen-Dazs, which has the most butterfat of all the ice creams, and Ben & Jerry's.

    1 cup cocoa
    1 cup light corn syrup
    2 plus 2 cups milk
    5 eggs
    2 cups sugar
    1 quart heavy whipping cream
    1 tablespoon vanilla extract

In saucepan combine cocoa, corn syrup, and 2 cups of milk. Bring to a boil over medium heat, stirring constantly. Cool completely. In mixing bowl beat eggs until foamy (about 5 minutes on high speed); gradually beat in sugar. Add cocoa mixture. Stir in remaining 2 cups milk, cream, and vanilla. Chill. Churn-freeze.

Place extra churned ice cream in freezer-safe container. Place piece of plastic wrap touching the ice cream and then place the lid over the wrap.

Makes 1 gallon—perfect for two light eaters

Note: We suggest you place these in 1-quart containers, and eat them directly out of the container. We recommend 2 quarts per person per sitting. Great on top of Pepperidge Farm Nantucket Cookies, with Hershey's Chocolate Sauce and a dollop of whipped cream.

APPLE DATE CAKE

My good friend Patricia Anderson made this cake for me once, and now it is my recipe for life. This is a family favorite, one that you will just absolutely love—even if your kids don't like dates, they will love this cake.

    2 Granny Smith and 2 Golden Delicious apples
 2 ½ cups all-purpose flour, divided
    1 cup finely chopped dates
 1 ½ cups chopped pecans
    2 sticks salted butter
    2 cups sugar
    2 eggs
    2 teaspoons ground cinnamon
    2 teaspoons baking soda
    1 teaspoon ground cloves
    ½ teaspoon salt

Preheat oven to 350 degrees. Grease and flour a tube pan. Peel, core, and chop the apples, and cook over medium heat until soft. Measure and keep 2 cups of apples hot on medium heat on the stove. Sprinkle 2 tablespoons of flour on the dates and pecans. With electric mixer, cream butter and sugar until light. Add eggs one at a time and beat until light and fluffy. Mix together flour, cinnamon, baking soda, cloves, and salt. Add dry ingredients to mixture a bit at a time; mix completely, but do not overbeat. Add the hot apples (don't worry, the mixture will look loose) and stir in dates and pecans. Bake for 1½ to 1¾ hours or until done. This cake is excellent by itself with a glass of sweet tea.

Cover with plastic wrap and keep in the refrigerator for at least 2 hours. Slice the cake with a serrated knife in 1½-inch pieces. Enjoy!

Makes 1 serving

SPANISH BAR CAKES

When we were kids, our family would drive from Florida to Boston and Maine to visit relatives. My dad would always stop at the A&P Grocery Store to purchase a dozen or so three-layer Spanish Bar Cakes. We no longer have an A&P in our state, and I'm not sure if they even still make Spanish Bar Cakes, so I tried to recreate the exact taste, and this is it. *You will love it!*

1 recipe Apple Date Cake (opposite page)

Frosting

3 sticks salted butter, room temperature
1 (8-ounce) package Philadelphia cream cheese, room temperature
2 teaspoons vanilla extract
7 cups (more if necessary) powdered sugar
Milk to make frosting consistency; start with 2 tablespoons and use more if necessary

Bake the Apple Date Cake in two loaf pans instead of one tube pan. Be sure to grease and flour the pans.

Make frosting. Cream butter and cream cheese until fluffy; add vanilla and sugar. Add enough milk to moisten and beat on high to make frosting easy to spread. Cut the cooled cake loaves in three vertical pieces (lengthwise). Liberally frost the bottom layer, then add the second and third layers, frosting between the layers and frosting the top and sides completely as well.

Makes 1 serving

AUNT HILDA'S BLUEBERRY CAKE RECIPE

My Uncle Bradford and Aunt Hilda had a dairy farm in Buckfield, Maine, right outside North Turner near Bear Pond. Every summer when we visited from Florida, my aunt would have this delicious warm cake ready for us, made with blueberries fresh from the field, picked by our cousins Ronnie and Priscilla.

2 ½ cups all-purpose flour, divided
1½ cups fresh blueberries (never canned—but you can use frozen)
½ cup (1 stick) butter
1½ cups sugar
2 eggs, beaten
½ teaspoon salt
1 teaspoon vanilla extract
1 tablespoon baking powder
1 cup milk
Granulated sugar for dusting

Preheat oven to 350 degrees. Mix ¼ cup of the flour with the blueberries. With electric mixer cream butter and sugar together; add the beaten eggs and beat until light and fluffy. Add the salt, vanilla, and baking powder. Add half the remaining flour and mix on low speed, adding half the milk, then the remaining flour and milk, in that order. Do not overmix. Fold in the blueberries. Dust the top with granulated sugar. Bake in a greased 9 x 13-inch (or smaller) pan for about 35 minutes. As soon as it comes out of the oven, liberally dust the top with more granulated sugar. Let it cool in the pan for 15 minutes—and eat warm. If there are any leftovers (and there shouldn't be!) cover with plastic wrap and store in the same pan.

Makes 2 servings

SOUTHERN PECAN PIE

People ask for this recipe every time this pie is served. You'll love it more than life itself. It's the easiest and best-tasting pecan pie you'll ever make.

      6 extra large eggs
    1⅓ cups granulated sugar
      ½ teaspoon salt
      ⅔ cup melted butter
      1 bottle Karo's light corn syrup (2 cups)
      2 cups quality whole pecans (pieces can be used, but whole pecans look nicer)
      1 (10-inch) piecrust (page 70)

Preheat oven to 450 degrees. In large mixing bowl, beat eggs with a whisk. Add sugar, salt, butter, and corn syrup and stir until well mixed. Add pecans and stir. Pour mixture into piecrust. Bake on bottom rack in the oven for 15 minutes. Reduce heat to 350 degrees and continue baking for 30 to 45 minutes or until pie is well set in the middle. If pecans seem to be browning too much, lightly place a sheet of aluminum foil on top of the pie while in the oven. Eat this pie at room temperature. Never refrigerate.

Varitions: For chocolate pecan pie, stir in 1 cup chocolate chip morsels. For bourbon pecan pie, stir in ½ cup Jack Daniels bourbon whisky. Or stir in both chocolate and bourbon and make bourbon chocolate pecan pie. But frankly, I like just plain old southern pecan pie. Try that first, then the variations if you wish.

THE PURPLE COW

This is the perfect bedtime drink.

16 ounces Welch's grape juice, cold
1 pint Häagen-Dazs vanilla ice cream

In a 32-ounce glass (a 7-11 Super Gulp cup is perfect), pour the Welch's grape juice until half full. Add one pint of Häagen-Dazs ice cream. Stir and drink with a straw.

Makes 1 serving

Variation: For a spritzer, add 3 ounces ginger ale or 7-Up.

I Never Saw a Purple Cow
I Never Hope To See One
But I can Tell You Now,
I'd Rather See Than Be One.

7-LAYER NABISCO ENGLISH TRIFLE

7 packages Jell-O instant vanilla pudding

4 containers Cool Whip

2 pounds Smuckers Raspberry Preserves

1 package Nabisco Mini Chips Ahoy cookies

1 package Nabisco Mini Teddy crackers

1 package Nabisco Mini Oreos

1 package Nabisco Mini Nutter Butters

1 package Nabisco Animal Crackers

1 package Nabisco Cameo Crème Cookies (crushed)

1 package Nabisco Nilla Wafers (whole for top of Trifle)

Make the Jell-O pudding according to package directions. In large punch bowl, place the first package of cookies on bottom, and layer with vanilla pudding, raspberry preserves, and Cool Whip. Keep adding cookies and layers of pudding, Cool Whip, and preserves until cookies are used up, finishing with the Nabisco Nilla Wafers. Cover with plastic wrap and chill overnight.

Makes 4 servings

FLOSSIE'S BEST-EVER PUMPKIN PIE

Most everyone says that their mom makes the best . . . whatever. I'm no different. My mom was one of the most giving people in my life. Each Thanksgiving and Christmas she would make "oodles and oodles" (her words) of ten-inch pumpkin pies to give to the neighbors. They were a smash hit. Now I continue the tradition, and everyone says these are the *best*!

Filling

    1 (32-ounce) can Libby's 100 percent pure pumpkin (not pumpkin pie mix)

    1 (15-ounce) can Libby's 100 percent pure pumpkin (not pumpkin pie mix)

    1 cup brown sugar (packed tightly)

1¼ cups granulated sugar

    1 tablespoon ground cinnamon

    1 tablespoon ground nutmeg

    ¼ teaspoon ground cloves

    1 teaspoon salt

    5 eggs, beaten

    5 cups whole milk, room temperature

Best Ever Piecrust

2⅔ cups all-purpose flour

    1 teaspoon salt

    2 sticks very cold salted butter, cubed

    8 tablespoons ice cold water

For the filling, combine all ingredients in large mixing bowl and stir with large spoon until well blended. You can use a store-bought pie shell, but if you're going this far, go all the way and make the crust too—it's simple!

For the piecrust, preheat the oven to 450 degrees. Put the flour and salt in a food processor with cubed butter (about 1-tablespoon chunks). Pulse about 10 times or until the flour is blended to a cornmeal consistency. Add the ice water and pulse another 6 to 12 times until it forms a ball. Divide in two even balls of pastry on a lightly floured surface. Roll to fit the size pie plate you are using, then fill the piecrust with even amounts of pumpkin filling. Bake on lowest rack in the oven for 15 minutes. Raise the rack to the middle of the oven, reduce the heat to 350 degrees, and continue baking for 40 to 60 minutes or until a butter knife inserted in the middle comes out clean. Let it cool completely, refrigerate, and serve cold.

Makes 2 servings

THE BEST OF THE BEST

Best Sugars: REFINED WHITE AND BROWN

Best Flour: PROCESSED ALL-PURPOSE WHITE

Best Fat For Frying: LARD

Best Fat For Flavor and Mass Consumption: BUTTER

Best Caloric Bread: BAGELS (THE LARGER THE BETTER)

Best Quick Meal Replacement: BAG OF PEPPERIDGE FARM SAUSALITO COOKIES

NEW ORLEANS BREAD PUDDING WITH WHISKEY ICING

This is one of my favorite desserts of all time. Some like it warm or hot; I like it ice cold. Serve with a whiskey sauce or our awesome Caramel Sauce. The choice is yours.

Bread Pudding

- 1 large loaf Pepperidge Farm white bread (about 25 to 35 large pieces)— or any other firm white bread
- 2 cups granulated sugar
- 1 teaspoon vanilla extract
- 2 teaspoons cinnamon (or more if desired)
- 3 eggs, beaten
- 1 quart whole milk, room temperature
- 4 tablespoons butter
- 1 cup raisins (more if desired)

Whiskey Topping

- 1 stick salted butter, room temperature
- 2 cups powdered sugar
  Maker's Mark whiskey

Caramel Sauce

- 1½ cups sugar
- ½ cup water
- 1 cup heavy cream, room temperature
- 1 stick salted butter

Preheat oven to 350 degrees. Cut all the crusts off the bread and put crustless bread in large mixing bowl. Combine all bread pudding ingredients in bowl with bread and stir until completely mixed. Place in buttered 9 x 13-inch baking dish. If you'd like a taller pudding, use a smaller dish. If you want a 1-inch pudding, use a full size cookie sheet with a 1-inch lip all around the sides (this size is perfect for cutting 1-inch squares for cocktail parties). Bake for 45 minutes to 1 hour, depending on the size of the pan. A knife inserted in the middle will come out fairly clean (not like a cake, but it won't stick too much) when done. If you are baking in a cookie sheet, check after 20 minutes of baking.

For whisky topping, beat together the butter and sugar with electric mixer. Add whiskey about 1 tablespoon at a time until desired consistency. We recommend a soft but firm icing-like consistency so you can put a small dollop on each slice. A glaze can be developed just by adding more whiskey.

For caramel sauce, in large saucepan or skillet, caramelize the sugar and water until it is a medium brown color. Remove from heat. Immediately add the room temperature cream, slowly whisking the entire time. Be careful of rising steam. Whisk in small pieces of butter. Pour over pudding, warm or cold.

Makes 2 to 3 servings

**"I've been on a diet two weeks,
and all I've lost is two weeks."
–Tootie Fields**

BETTER-THAN-OLD-FASHIONED BANANA CAKE

 5 large bananas, very ripe
 1 stick salted butter
 2 cups sugar
 2 eggs
 ¼ teaspoon salt
 1 teaspoon baking soda
 1 teaspoon vanilla extract
 ¼ cup buttermilk
 2½ cups sifted all-purpose flour

Preheat oven to 375 degrees. Use butter or Crisco to grease and flour a tube pan or two bread loaf pans. Peel bananas and beat with an electric mixer until completely mashed. In separate mixer, cream butter and sugar, add eggs one at a time, and beat with electric mixer until light and fluffy. Add salt, baking soda, vanilla, and buttermilk and beat until blended. Add mashed bananas and beat for about 1 minute or until blended. Add flour in two parts and beat until mixed. Be careful not to overmix flour or cake will be tough.

We recommend that you bake in a tube pan but loaf pans will do. If baking in a tube pan, bake for exactly 1 hour or until a toothpick stuck in the center comes out clean. Remove from the pan and let cool before cutting. Great served the next day. Very good served warm with chilled whipped cream and sliced bananas.

Makes 2 servings

FRENCH MARKET BEIGNETS (DOUGHNUTS)

Homemade doughnuts are the best. And homemade beignets are the best of the best. This recipe was given to me twenty years ago by a good friend who got it from a friend who got it from the *River Road Cookbook*. These beat even the beignets served at cafés in New Orleans.

1 cup whole milk

¼ cup granulated sugar

¾ teaspoon salt

½ teaspoon ground nutmeg

1 package active dry yeast

2 tablespoons lukewarm water

2 tablespoons vegetable oil

1 egg, beaten

3½ cups all-purpose flour, sifted

Lots of confectioner's sugar

1 medium-size paper bag

Scald the milk in a saucepan over medium heat. Add the granulated sugar, salt, and nutmeg. Cool to lukewarm. Sprinkle or crumble the yeast into the lukewarm water, stirring until yeast is dissolved. To the lukewarm milk mixture add the oil, egg, and dissolved yeast and blend with a spoon. Gradually add the flour, beating well. Cover with wax paper and a clean towel and let rise in warm place until double in size.

Turn the dough (it will be soft) onto a well-floured surface; knead gently. Roll into an 18 x 12-inch rectangle; cut into 36 (3-inch) squares. Cover with a clean towel and let rise for 30 minutes.

Preheat a fryer to 375 degrees. Fry a few doughnuts at a time in the fryer until golden brown. Drain on crumpled paper towels. Drop the doughnuts in the brown paper bag loaded with confectioners' sugar and shake until thoroughly coated. Serve hot.

Makes 6 servings (6 doughnuts per serving)

Note: Always serve hot out of the fryer, sprinkled liberally with confectioners' sugar. These are not good cold or left over—as if you would have any left over!

Chapter Five

OUR SANDWICH BAR

An important culinary note: The sandwiches listed here should be enjoyed with a thick and rich chocolate shake, a squirt of whipped cream, a Maraschino cherry, and of course, a large order of french fries covered with warm Cheez Whiz. If you happen to be in the Tampa, Florida, area, we recommend finishing lunch off with the largest (and best-tasting) piece of homemade coconut cream pie you'll ever eat, made by Marc and Dede Zudar at Zudar's Deli.

SPAM AND PORK AND BEAN FOCACCIA

Created by Kevin and Karyn Kruszewski
Proprietors of the awesome Pane Rustica Bakery and Café, Tampa, Florida, home of great bread and huge portions.

- 1 can Hormel SPAM
- 1 can Bush's barbecue baked beans
- 2 slices sun-dried tomato and basil focaccia bread

Layer thick slices of the SPAM alternately with the baked beans onto fresh, thick-sliced focaccia bread. Liberally butter outsides of the bread and grill on an indoor grill.

Makes 1 serving

JALAPEÑO WRAP

3 tablespoons tarragon-infused butter

1 large flour tortilla

3 tablespoons chunky peanut butter

1 pound applewood smoked bacon

8 slices jalapeño American cheese

2 avocados, sliced

Liberally spread the tarragon–infused butter on the tortilla. Spread the peanut butter on top of the butter layer. Add the thick sliced bacon, jalapeño cheese, and avocado slices. Roll tightly and cut diagonally. Serve with a bowl of warm canned creamed corn for dipping.

Makes 1 serving

POTATO CHIP AND MIRACLE WHIP SANDWICH

This delicious sandwich was a staple at my pal Stephen Crawford's house while I was growing up. His mom had these ready for us every day after kindergarten. Even though we now recommend serving this sandwich with a chocolate milkshake and cheese fries, she served them with an ice cold cherry coke and piping hot Campbell's tomato soup made with heavy cream. She even crushed extra potato chips in the soup. What a caring mom!

1 tablespoon Miracle Whip

2 slices white bread

3 ounces crushed Lay's potato chips

Spread the Miracle Whip on both slices of the bread. Feel free to add more to your taste. Sprinkle the potato chips on one slice of bread. Be careful as you pile them on so they don't spill. Put the second slice on top of the mound of chips and press with your hand to secure the chips in place. Enjoy!

Makes 1 serving

TRIPLE-DECKER MAMA CASS ELLIOT HAM SANDWICH

3 tablespoons butter, softened

1 French baguette, cut lengthwise

3 tablespoons mayonnaise

1 pound Capacola (Italian ham), sliced thin

1 pound Gruyère cheese, grated

1 pound Tavern ham, sliced thin

1 to 2 gherkin pickles, sliced lengthwise

1 pound oven-roasted maple-glazed ham

12 ounces Kraft American cheese (about 6 slices)

Liberally spread the butter on one side of the baguette and the mayonnaise on the other. Place the Capacola on one baguette slice. Continue by layering the Gruyère cheese and Tavern ham, followed by gherkin pickles, oven-roasted ham, and, finally, the Kraft American cheese. This goes great with a bag of Oreos, a gallon of Grape Kool-Aid, and a family-size bag of Fritos.

Makes 1 serving

Note: All ham should be Boar's Head and sliced paper thin. *Caution:* Do not eat in bed.

CRACKED WHEAT BREAD

This dense cracked wheat bread is *super* and will be a delight to everyone who tries it as a sandwich or just toasted with butter and marmalade. Many think homemade bread making is difficult. It is not. Note: This recipe is *not* for bread machines. You must do it the old-fashioned way.

    2 cups boiling water
 1¼ cups cracked wheat (bulgur wheat)
    2 tablespoons butter
 ½ cup brown sugar
    2 teaspoons salt
    2 packages dry granule yeast
 ⅔ cup warm water
    1 tablespoon granulated sugar
 3 ¾ cups sifted bread flour (more if necessary)

Pour the boiling water over the cracked wheat. Add the butter, brown sugar, and salt. Set aside until cool. Dissolve the yeast in the warm water and add granulated sugar. Set aside. If the yeast is good, it should begin to foam in 3 to 5 minutes. (If it doesn't, you need to go to the store and buy more.) Add the yeast to the cooled cracked wheat. Place the cooled cracked wheat mixture in a large mixing bowl and add the flour. Mix until it forms a pliable ball. It should not be sticky. You may need to add extra flour, a little at a time until the desired consistency is reached.

Turn the dough out onto a floured surface and knead until smooth. Place it in a buttered bowl, cover the top of the bowl with a clean dish towel, and let the dough rise for 1 hour. Punch down and let it rise again for 30 minutes. Punch down again and turn the dough onto a floured surface. Shape it into 2 loaves. Place the dough into greased (not buttered) loaf pans and let it rise until it reaches the tops of the pans. Preheat the oven to 350 degrees.

Bake for 1 hour and 15 minutes. Once the bread is done, immediately take out of the pans and let it cool on a baking rack for at least 15 minutes before cutting—if you can wait that long!

Chapter Six

VEGETABLES: HOW THEY SHOULD BE EATEN!

The best vegetables to ensure maximum success on the North Beach Diet are potatoes and corn. Yes, there are other vegetables you can consume on our program, and we have found a great many pastas infused with them. So if you must eat vegetables other than potatoes and corn, eat pasta infused with vegetables. We recommend pasta made with carrots (good for eyesight) and spinach (good for strength), which can be purchased at any quality grocery store. If you can find cheese tortellini made with vegetable pasta, you'll have the best of all three worlds: pasta, vegetables, and cheese.

An Important Dietary Note

We highly recommend that both potatoes and corn be served at every meal. We have provided a few of our favorite recipes for your enjoyment. But don't stop with these—create your own dishes. However, if you are short on time, a can of creamed corn and a bag of frozen french fries will do just fine.

BISCUITS AND CHOCOLATE GRAVY

You're probably saying to yourself right now: "What? Biscuits and chocolate gravy ain't vegetables." And you're right. But when we were knee-high to a leg of lamb, my daddy always told us, "Biscuits and chocolate gravy is vegetables." And we believed him right up until the age of nineteen or so.

Homemade biscuits are best, but we also recommend the large biscuits from KFC or Popeye's restaurants. Biscuits should be cut in half and served warm with chocolate gravy.

Southern Buttermilk Biscuits

- 2 cups all-purpose flour
- 2 teaspoons baking powder
- ½ teaspoon baking soda
- 1 tablespoon granulated sugar
- 1 teaspoon salt
- 1 stick cold salted butter, cubed
- ¾ cup cold full cultured buttermilk (no reduced fat)

Chocolate Gravy

- 2 tablespoons butter
- 3 tablespoons all-purpose flour
- 4 tablespoons sugar
- 2 tablespoons cocoa powder
- 2 cups milk
- 1 teaspoon vanilla extract

Preheat oven to 450 degrees and place a rack in the center of the oven. In a food processor add the flour, baking powder, baking soda, sugar, and salt, and pulse 3 times to combine. Add cubes of cold butter and pulse until totally incorporated into the flour mixture (like cornmeal consistency). Pour the mixture into a mixing bowl and add the buttermilk. Mix with a fork (or your hands) until combined. Be careful not to overmix or the biscuits will be tough.

Place the dough on a floured surface and roll out to 1 inch thickness. With a biscuit cutter, cut to the size you desire. Reform the dough only one more time; after that, the biscuits will get tough. Place the biscuits on a parchment–lined aluminum baking sheet. (Note: Never use a dark baking sheet for baking anything, especially biscuits and cookies, because they can burn your product quickly.) Brush the tops of the biscuits with melted butter. Depending on the size of the biscuit, bake for 10 to 20 minutes. If the biscuits are small, check after 8 minutes; for larger ones, check after 10 minutes. Bake until golden brown. Brush again with melted butter.

For gravy, in a 2-quart saucepan, melt the butter over medium heat, add the flour and stir with a whisk for approximately 5 minutes. Add the sugar and cocoa powder and then the milk about ¼ cup at a time, stirring constantly over medium heat. Once thickened, take off the stove and add the vanilla. Cool to warm and serve over biscuits.

Makes 4 breakfast servings or 2 midnight snack servings

Variation: You can make cheddar cheese biscuits by decreasing the butter to 5 tablespoons and adding 1 cup grated extra-sharp cheddar cheese at the same time as the butter.

WARNING TO PARENTS!
New Link Found Between Thinness and Cereal Killers

What did Adolf Hitler, Ted Bundy, Stuart Whidden, Jack the Ripper, Charles Manson, and Lizzie Borden have in common? They were all thin. It took us by surprise as well. However, noted criminologist Dr. Stephen Robert Cribb, PhD, a crime fighter who has single-handedly captured more cereal killers than even J. Edgar Hoover, and is currently dean of students at the Institute for the Criminally Insane, located at the University of South Brandon outside Tampa, Florida, has found the link to end all speculation.

Dr. Cribb writes in an article for the October 2002 issue of the *New England Journal of Criminal Behavior:* "The evidence is overwhelming: 98 percent of all mass murderers and cereal killers (in all of history), were committed by the thin."

After studying the stomachs of twenty-seven mass murderers, Dr. Cribb said in an interview on the *Ricki Lake Show:* "We recommend a diet high in refined sugars, carbohydrates, and fat, to offset the dangers associated with being thin . . . virtually eliminating the likelihood of your thin child becoming a cereal killer." He continued: "An obese child is less likely to become a significant danger to society"

Need we say more?

CORN CASSEROLE

You will love every single bite of this delicious corn casserole. It goes well with everything from our southern fried chicken to our Cognac-Braised Short Ribs. Make sure you serve a potato dish alongside—remember, you should always have at least two vegetables at every meal.

1 medium onion	¼ cup sugar
½ stick butter, melted	1 cup sour cream
1 can whole kernel corn	1 box Jiffy corn muffin mix
1 can creamed corn	

Preheat oven to 350 degrees. In skillet over medium heat, sauté onion in melted better until translucent. Place corn, creamed corn, sugar, sour cream, and corn muffin mix in large mixing bowl and stir until well mixed. Pour into buttered casserole dish and bake for 30 to 45 minutes, or until light golden brown. This recipe can be doubled or tripled.

Makes 2 servings

BUTTERY CORN ON THE COB

Typically, ears of corn are boiled in water, but we recommend replacing the water with butter. Place ten pounds of salted butter in a large heavy-bottomed pot and melt over medium-low heat. Add as many shucked and washed ears of corn as you desire, and cook (covered) over medium-low heat for approximately one hour or until tender, depending on how many ears of corn you are cooking. This will be at a low simmer, not boiling; if the heat is too high, you'll burn the butter. Salt each cooked ear to taste and serve piping hot. This corn is good reheated.

The remaining butter can be drizzled over the corn, and can be kept for up to a week in the refrigerator for use in casseroles and other dishes throughout the week. It has a wonderful taste, and will never go to waste.

AUTHENTIC LOUISIANA RED BEANS AND RICE

You've never tasted better red beans and rice, even in Louisiana. They go great with anything or just in a big bowl by themselves. They are especially good with fried shrimp or pork chops.

    4 medium onions, chopped
    8 scallions (green onions), chopped
    1 large green pepper
    1 large ham hock
    8 ounces diced ham from the butcher (not the kind you'll find in the deli)
    3 cups dried red beans, drained and soaked overnight
    1 tablespoon salt
    5 cloves fresh garlic
    1 cup chopped parsley
    1 teaspoon cayenne pepper (or more to taste)
    1 teaspoon black pepper
    1 teaspoon Tabasco
    3 tablespoons Lea & Perrins Worcestershire sauce
    1 (16-ounce) can crushed tomatoes
    1 small can tomato paste
    ½ teaspoon dried oregano
    ½ teaspoon dried thyme
      Water or canned chicken stock

In a large pot, sauté the onions, green pepper, ham hock, and diced ham over medium heat until soft. Add drained soaked beans, then the remaining ingredients. Add 2 quarts water or chicken stock, enough so the beans are covered more than 2 inches. Put a lid on the pot and bring to a rapid boil. Stir from the bottom of the pot. Turn the heat to medium low, cover the pot, and cook for 2 to 3 hours or until the beans are tender to the bite. Stir occasionally to make sure beans do not stick to the bottom of the pot. Serve in a bowl over white rice.

Makes 1 serving

★ OUR GENERAL STORE ★

NORTH BEACH DIET PRODUCTS FOR PETS

Are You Worried About Your Pets Not Being Corpulent?
NBD Has the Answer for You

INTRODUCING

PURINA'S Puppy Chow Mien
They'll Be Hungry Every Two Hours

Doggie Downers
"You'll Never Have to Walk Your Dog Again"
Designer Sedatives to Slow Your Dogs Metabolism

IAMS Franco-American Spaghetti-Os
It's Not Just for People Anymore

Ritz Cheese Stuffs for Birds
Polly No Longer Wants Just a Plain Cracker
Turn Little Birdie into Big Bird

Lane Bryant Animal Fashions
Keep Your Fad-Crazed Plus-Size Pet in Vogue

PETA Approved – Pets Have Rights Too

NBD GENERAL STORE

www.northbeachdietonline.com

We Accept Diners Club Card Only

DELICIOUS NEW ENGLAND CORN CHOWDER

My mom used to have this hot delicious corn chowder ready for us to eat as soon as we got off the bus from school . . . she would serve this with a triple grilled cheese (American, cheddar, and Swiss), mayo, and sweet pickle sandwich. We'd eat this around four o'clock in the afternoon, two or three hours before dinner so as not to disturb our appetite. What a mom! She was always looking out for us.

       6 slices bacon, diced
       2 medium onions
       2 sticks salted butter
       1 cup all-purpose flour
    1½ to 2 quarts whole milk
       3 cans creamed corn
       3 cans corn kernels, drained
       ½ cup sugar
       6 medium-sized red new potatoes (peeled, cubed in small chunks,
          and boiled in salted water until done)
          Salt and pepper

In a large heavy saucepan, fry bacon (finely cubed salt pork can be used instead of bacon if desired) until crispy. Add chopped onions and butter, and cook until onions are soft and translucent. Add 1 cup of flour and constantly stir until a nice roux is made—light brown. On medium-high heat, add milk about 2 cups at a time, stirring constantly until thick. Add corn, sugar, and potatoes. Salt and pepper to taste.

Bring almost to a boil, but under no circumstances let it boil or it will curdle. Turn off, let cool completely, then reheat and serve. This is even better made a day in advance.

Makes 2 servings

CHEDDAR CHEESY HASH BROWNS WITH SOUR CREAM

Wait until you taste these potatoes—and they are so easy to make.

2 ½ cups extra sharp cheddar cheese
1 stick salted butter plus some for greasing the pan
1 cup sour cream
⅓ cup minced onion
1 (2-pound) package frozen hash brown potatoes (the fresh packaged kind you find in the dairy case are even better)
Salt and pepper
Paprika

Preheat oven to 350 degrees. Butter an 8-inch-square baking dish. Cook 2 cups cheese and butter in a large heavy saucepan over low heat until almost melted, stirring constantly, about 1 minute. Remove from heat. Stir in sour cream and onion. Add potatoes and season with salt and pepper to taste. Fold cheese mixture with the potatoes. Pour into buttered dish. Top with remaining ½ cup cheese and sprinkle with paprika. Bake until bubbly, about 30 minutes.

Makes only 1 serving, so you had better triple up on the recipe.

POTATOES: APPLES OF THE EARTH

The French call them *pommes de terre* (apples of the earth); we call them just plain "good eatin'." As we have noted, potatoes should be served with every meal. Whether it's hash browns for breakfast, french fries for lunch, or simple mashed potatoes at dinner, there are thousands of ways to prepare potatoes for your family and friends.

For a special celebration dinner, we suggest that you try serving just potatoes, preparing them five or six different ways. Serve your potato dinner with homemade potato garlic bread and sweet tea, and you'll have a meal fit for a king.

GORGONZOLA AND BALSAMIC PORTABELLA MUSHROOM POTATO SALAD

While we have nothing against the typical potato salad, our family wanted a change, so we created this incredible tasting salad. It is perfect for any outdoor occasion.

    5 pounds red new potatoes
    ½ cup Chardonnay
      Salt and pepper
    ¼ plus ¼ cup (1 stick) butter
    1 pound baby portabella mushrooms
    2 garlic cloves, minced
    3 tablespoons balsamic vinegar
 1¼ cup Hellmann's mayonnaise
 1¼ cup sour cream
 2½ tablespoons Dijon mustard
 2½ tablespoons red wine vinegar
    ¾ pound crumbled Gorgonzola cheese
    5 green onions
 1½ cups finely chopped celery

Place whole (washed and cleaned) unpeeled potatoes in a large heavy pot, cover with cold water, and boil until tender. Drain. Cool slightly, but not all the way—you want them warm. Cut into 1-inch pieces. Transfer to large bowl, add the wine, and season with salt and pepper to taste. Toss to coat well. Melt ½ stick butter in a frying pan until extremely hot, but not burnt. Add the mushrooms and stir. Add garlic cloves and vinegar, and cook over high heat until mushrooms absorb all the liquid and the mushrooms brown well. Combine all the remaining ingredients and mix with the potatoes and mushrooms. Adjust salt and pepper if needed. Cover and refrigerate. Let stand approximately 30 minutes at room temperature before serving.

Makes 4 servings

A TASTY DIP FOR FRENCH FRIES

Let's start with everyone's favorite, french fries. While we thoroughly enjoy ketchup on our french fries, we have created a dip that you and your friends will just love.

        1 cup Hellmann's mayonnaise
        ½ cup Heinz ketchup
        2 tablespoons honey
        1 bulb oven-roasted garlic, mashed*
        1 teaspoon Lea & Perrins Worcestershire sauce
        ½ teaspoon kosher salt
        ½ teaspoon ground cayenne

In a medium size mixing bowl whisk together the mayonnaise, ketchup, honey, garlic, Worcestershire sauce, salt, and cayenne. As with all recipes, add or subtract according to your desired taste. If you like it spicier, add some Tabasco or finely chopped jalapeño peppers; if you'd like it a bit sweeter add more honey or ketchup—you decide. But we guarantee you'll love this dipping sauce with french fries or even fried fish.

Makes 2 servings

Note: To prepare oven-roasted garlic: Cut the entire top off a garlic bulb, drizzle with olive oil, and sprinkle with kosher salt. Tightly wrap in aluminum foil and bake at 400 degrees for 30 to 40 minutes. You can bake multiple bulbs at one time. Oven-roasted garlic is awesome mixed with butter as a spread for bread, or even added to mashed potatoes.

OVERSTUFFED TWICE BAKED POTATOES

    1 large baking potato
    ½ cup (1 stick) plus 2 tablespoons butter, melted
    ¼ cup heavy cream
    ½ teaspoon salt
    1 teaspoon Lea & Perrins Worcestershire sauce
    ½ teaspoon black pepper
    1 whole green onion (scallion), finely chopped
    2 slices Kraft American cheese
    2 ounces Cracker Barrel extra sharp cheddar cheese

Buy the largest baking potatoes you can find. Wash and bake at 400 degrees until done, usually about an hour (this depends on how large the potato is and how many are in the oven).

While still hot, cut in half. Using a pot holder, hold each half and scoop out the inside potato with a tablespoon, leaving ⅛ inch of the potato clinging to the inside skin. Brush the inside skin with 2 tablespoons melted butter and salt.

Reduce the oven to 375 degrees. Add to the hot potato the stick of salted butter, heavy cream, salt, Worcestershire sauce, black pepper, green onion, American cheese, and cheddar cheese. Mash with potato masher, fork, or with an electric mixer. Stuff mixture into empty potato shells, dot with butter, and sprinkle with paprika. Bake for 30 minutes.

Makes 1 serving

Note: According to Bradford and Hilda Beedy, dairy farmers from Buckfield, Maine, "Always use heavy cream and real butter in your mashed potatoes."

STUPENDOUSLY DELICIOUS
SCALLOPED POTATOES

This dish is made with sweet potatoes (or yams) and regular white potatoes.

> 6 large sweet potatoes, peeled
> 8 large baking potatoes, sliced into ¼-inch rounds
> ½ cup (1 stick) butter, soft, not melted
>   Salt and pepper
> 9 tablespoons minced shallots
> 1½ pounds grated Gruyère cheese
> 1 quart heavy cream
> 2 cups freshly grated Parmesan cheese (never the canned stuff)
> 2 cups plain bread crumbs

Parboil the potatoes until just about done. Let cool. Preheat oven to 375 degrees. Liberally butter a large baking dish. Layer the dish with sweet potatoes, dots of the soft butter, salt and pepper to taste, 3 table-spoons minced shallots, and lots of grated Gruyère cheese. Do the same with the regular white potatoes, and keep layering until all the potatoes are used. Cover with 1 quart of heavy cream. Mix together the freshly grated Parmesan cheese and the plain bread crumbs and spread over the top of the potatoes. Bake for approximately 90 minutes or until bubbly hot, gooey, and golden brown. Let cool 15 minutes before serving.

Makes 2 servings

FIVE TIPS FOR QUALITY EATING

1) Never Buy or Cook with Organic Products
2) Never use Sugar or Fat Substitutes
3) Eat Fruits in Pies and Desserts Only
4) Eat Vegetables Fried or in Casseroles Loaded with Cheese Sauce
5) Before Presenting a Dish for Consumption, Look for Ways to Add Calories—Like Adding Ice Cream to Desserts and Butter to Everything Else

THE BEST TASTIN' SALSA ON EARTH

This salsa recipe was contributed by two of Mexico's most accomplished chefs: Elisa Ramirez and Gerarda Tapia.

    6 large vine ripe tomatoes, cut in quarters
    3 green onions (scallions)
    2 large whole jalapeño peppers (including vein and seeds)
    1 cup fresh cilantro
    ½ large green bell pepper
    ½ medium red onion
    3 large garlic cloves
    2 tablespoons red wine vinegar
    3 tablespoons fresh (never bottled) lime juice
    2 tablespoons extra-virgin olive oil
    ½ cup tomato paste
    1 teaspoon salt (or more to taste)
    2 mangoes

In a food processor, pulse the tomatoes. Remove and set aside in large bowl. To the food processor add the onions, jalapeño peppers, cilantro, green bell pepper, red onion, and garlic. Pulse chop and add to the chopped tomatoes, along with the red wine vinegar, lime juice, olive oil, tomato paste, and salt. Pulse chop entire mixture (in batches) 6 to 10 times each batch or until you reach the desired consistency. At the very end, roughly chop the mangoes and toss into finished salsa. This salsa is best if made 3 to 6 hours ahead. Keep refrigerated. Eat with lots of restaurant style chips—lime-scented chips are especially good with this salsa.

Makes about 12 cups or 2 servings

Note: Our Mexican chefs say that the key component to creating an *awesome* tasting salsa is to completely understand and comprehend the following: *Es que nunca le des instrucciones a los gringos en ningun otro lenguage que el ingles; ellos no lo pueden a similar.*

DARN GOOD QUICHE

Even men will eat this quiche. In Texas, a man will have to go behind the barn to eat typical quiche—but he can eat this quiche right out in front of all his dudes without blinking an eye. It's the best quiche you'll ever taste.

2 (9-inch) pie shells	4 eggs, beaten
½ pound crispy bacon	2 ½ cups heavy cream
1 stick salted butter, divided	1½ cups Gruyère cheese, grated
1 large onion, chopped	1½ cups Asiago cheese, grated
1 pound mushrooms, chopped	¼ cup Parmesan cheese, grated
1 teaspoon salt, divided	¼ teaspoon ground nutmeg
½ teaspoon cayenne	½ teaspoon fine ground pepper
2 tablespoons high quality balsamic vinegar	

Preheat oven to 450 degrees. Line two 9-inch pie pans with homemade or store-bought pie shells. Flute edges, poke entire pie shell with a fork to keep from crust bubbling up while baking, and bake for 5 minutes. While pie shells are baking, fry bacon until crisp, then crumble. Melt ½ stick butter in skillet and sauté onion until soft and translucent. Remove from skillet, and add the remaining ½ stick of butter, melt the butter until the pan is fire hot and the butter begins to brown (but not burn), then toss in chopped mushrooms. Add ½ teaspoon salt, cayenne, and balsamic vinegar. Fry on high heat until all the liquid has evaporated.

In medium bowl, beat eggs with a whisk, add cream, and whisk again until completely mixed. Strain this mixture into a large mixing bowl through a fine strainer to remove all egg particles. Add all the cheeses, nutmeg, and pepper, and stir until well combined. Bake for 15 minutes. Lower the temperature to 350 degrees and bake for 30 to 45 minutes longer, until it is nicely browned and a knife inserted in the middle comes out clean. The bottom of the quiche should be browned as well.

Makes 2 regular servings or 1 Texas-size serving

Variation: Lightly brush about 15 asparagus with extra-virgin olive oil, and a bit of salt and pepper. Bake at 450 degrees for 3 to 5 minutes only . . . you want them to be bright green out of the oven. Remove from heat and pan, and chop into ¼-inch pieces. Add to quiche mixture. (Despite this being a low-calorie vegetable, we love asparagus in quiche so much we still recommend it.)

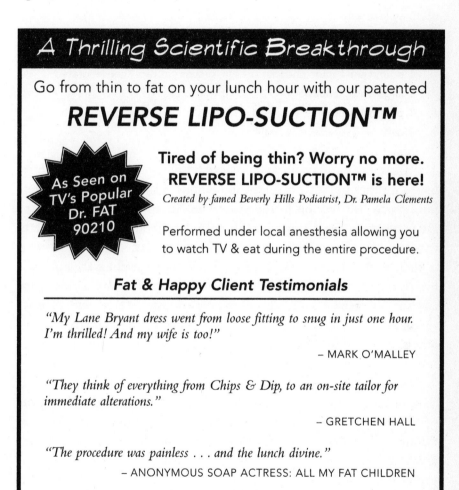

YELLOW SQUASH CASSEROLE

Perfect for a holiday meal side dish. Yes, it's a yellow vegetable, but with enough butter, cheese, and bread crumbs to make it worthwhile.

15 large yellow summer squash (washed, dried, cut in 1-inch chunks)
5 stalks celery
1 large onion or 2 medium onions
1 stick butter
1 pound extra sharp cheddar cheese, grated
2 large eggs, beaten
   Salt and pepper
2 cups unflavored bread crumbs

It's best if you can steam these vegetables all together, but if you don't have a steamer, put squash, celery, and onions in large pot and add water until pot is half way up to the vegetables. Steam or boil until tender. Drain all water from vegetables in colander (about 5 minutes); there should be absolutely no water left in the vegetables.

Preheat the oven to 350 degrees. While the vegetables are hot, add butter and cheese, and stir without crushing the vegetables. Add eggs and stir fast. Flavor with salt and pepper to taste—begin with ½ teaspoon each. Stir, but don't crush the vegetables. Place in buttered casserole dish, top with bread crumbs, and bake for 30 to 45 minutes.

Makes a couple servings

Variations: Zucchini can be used instead of the yellow squash, or you can use half zucchini and half yellow squash. And instead of an all bread crumb topping, mix 1 cup freshly grated Parmesan cheese with 1 cup plain bread crumbs.

Chapter Seven

THE MAIN COURSE

We offer you the following menu: Baked Free Range Chicken Stuffed with Tofu and Sprouts, Drizzled with a Reduced Vegetable Stock, a hint of Fresh Rosemary, and a touch of Lemon Scented Nonfat Yogurt Served on a Bed of Fresh Organic Eggplant, Tomatoes, and Zucchini Sautéd in Pam Nonfat Cooking Spray.

Yeah, right—what do you think this is, a joke book? Let's get down to some real food!

BACON RICE AND BEANS

   2 pounds bacon
   2 cups white rice
   4 cans Bush's pinto beans
   ½ cup chopped scallions
   1 pound cheddar cheese, grated

Fry the bacon until crisp and reserve the fat. Cook the rice per package instructions: typically 2 cups of water and 1 teaspoon of salt for every 1 cup of uncooked rice. Once the rice is cooked add crumbled bacon. In saucepan, heat the pinto beans and scallions with the fat of the bacon. Spoon the beans over the rice and top with the grated cheddar cheese. Serve with Maytag Blue Cheese Mashed Potatoes (page 101) and cornbread.

Makes 2 servings

BREAKFAST FOR DINNER

- Pancakes, Waffles, French Toast
- Ham and Potato Hash
- Fried Eggs, Grits, and Buttermilk Biscuits

Homemade or any type of frozen pancakes, waffles, and French toast will do—just make sure you cook plenty of anything. Serve with lots of bottled maple syrup and soft butter.

Fry as many eggs as you desire, using the bacon fat you've reserved from previous cooking. If you have none, fry up a pound, and throw the cooked bacon into the cooked grits, using the fat for frying the eggs. We recommend that eggs should never be fried in any fat other than bacon fat.

The Key to the Best Most Deliciously Creamy Grits Ever

Any brand of grits will do—we prefer the long cook method, but the quick cooked kind will do just fine—but never use instant. Cook grits according to the instructions on the package with two exceptions: 1) You must add more salt than called for, and 2) you must (yes, must) add half a stick of butter to the boiling water for every third of a cup of uncooked grits. This is a must.

Many southern cooks will use milk or cream instead of water. Even though we love milk and heavy cream, water is always best for cooking grits, especially when you are adding butter to the water during the cooking process. Serve piping hot with more butter and salt.

Note: You may add any type of cheese you desire: A sharp cheddar is always good, and crumbled bacon is good too.

HAM AND POTATO HASH

1½ cups (3 sticks) butter

3 (1-pound) bags cubed precooked potatoes (not frozen—these are typically found in the egg section of a major grocery store)

2 pounds Boar's Head Tavern ham (have deli cut into 1-pound thick slices), cubed

Salt and pepper

1 teaspoon paprika

In a heavy skillet, melt butter and add potatoes and cubed ham. Add salt and pepper to taste and paprika, and stir until well mixed. Let fry over medium-high heat until a golden brown crust forms, then flip to do the same on the other side.

Makes about 3 servings

MAYTAG BLUE CHEESE MASHED POTATOES

5 pounds red potatoes

3 cups (6 sticks) salted butter

1 pound Maytag blue cheese

Heavy cream for desired consistency

Salt and pepper

Boil the potatoes in salted water until fork tender. Drain, add the butter, blue cheese, and enough heavy cream to make a creamy mashed potato, beginning with ¾ cup. Mash until you reach the desired consistency. Season with salt and pepper to taste.

Makes 2 comfortable servings

FRIED PORK CHOPS WITH VELVEETA CHEESE SAUCE

10 pounds pork chops
5 pounds Velveeta cheese
2 ½ cups heavy cream

Coat pork chops according to the Ultimate Fried Anything directions on page 117. Fry pork chops in 1 inch vegetable oil over medium-high heat until golden brown, about 5 minutes per side. Wrap fried pork chops tightly in aluminum foil, and place in a 350-degree oven for 1 hour. These will be the tenderest pork chops you'll ever taste.

Melt Velveeta cheese in the microwave with heavy cream. You may have to melt this in batches. Use ½ cup cream for every pound of cheese. Stir every 3 minutes during the cooking process. Pour the cheese sauce over pork chops.

Makes 2 servings

Note: If you ever eat vegetables such as broccoli and cauliflower (and we don't know why you'd want to when you have potatoes and corn so readily available), liberally cover them in this cheese sauce.

VODKA PASTA

This pasta sauce has such a gourmet flavor you want to serve it to all your guests. The alcohol burns out, but the calories remain.

½ cup (1 stick) salted butter
6 whole shallots, finely chopped
3 (32-ounce) cans crushed tomatoes
1 cup heavy cream, room temperature
1 tablespoon sugar
   Salt
1 teaspoon red pepper flakes
1 cup high quality vodka
2 pounds penne pasta, cooked according to directions and drained

In a large heavy skillet, melt the butter and sauté the shallots until soft. Add the tomatoes and cook for 20 minutes over medium-high heat. Add the heavy cream, sugar, salt to taste, and pepper flakes. When hot and bubbling (not boiling), add the vodka and cook another 10 minutes. Serve over pasta with fresh Italian bread and flavored olive oil.

Makes 4 lunch servings, 2 dinner servings, or 1 evening snack serving

Note: To make the Italian bread mix 1 cup extra-virgin olive oil, ½ teaspoon salt, 1 teaspoon red pepper flakes, 1 teaspoon dried oregano, 1 teaspoon dried basil in a bottle with a tightly secured lid and shake vigorously. Spread on sliced bread and toast.

BUTTERMILK VIDALIA ONION RINGS

    2 extra-large Vidalia onions, peeled and sliced very thin
    1 quart buttermilk (not low fat)
    4 cups all-purpose flour
      Salt
      Black pepper
      Cayenne
      Lard, peanut, or vegetable oil for deep fat frying

Place thin onion slices in large bowl and coat with buttermilk and let sit for 1 hour in the refrigerator. Flavor the flour with salt, pepper, and cayenne to taste. Don't be afraid to add lots of each. Shake the buttermilk off the onions and coat with flour (a plastic baggie is good for this)—shake excess flour off rings and fry in hot oil (350 to 375 degrees) until golden brown and crispy. Place on rack covered with paper towels, and salt to taste while they are hot.

Makes 1 serving

PAN SEARED RIB-EYE STEAK

Next to outdoor grilling with charcoal (not gas), this will be your absolute favorite way to cook a streak. For me, rib eye is the best cut, with a tenderloin filet coming in a close second. However, any steak can be prepared like this. You will never go back to the way you were fixing steaks.

    1 (16-ounce or more) 2-inch rib-eye steak per person
    Salt and pepper
    Salted butter, room temperature
    2 garlic cloves, crushed

Rub the steak liberally with salt and pepper to taste, and generously rub with the butter until steak is totally coated. Get a cast-iron skillet very hot. Throw that steak in the pan. *Do not*, repeat, *do not* touch the steak for at least 3 minutes. Also, never—that's *never*—poke a steak with a fork to turn it; always use tongs.

Preheat oven to 450 degrees. Turn the steak and cook for another 3 minutes. Remove from the stove and add 2 tablespoons of butter in the pan along with garlic. Place the entire pan in the oven for 5 minutes for rare or longer until it is cooked the way you prefer—hopefully not well done. Remove the steak from the skillet and let it rest on a warmed plate (loosely covered) for 8 to 10 minutes.

Makes 1 serving

Note: Never cut a steak as soon as it's taken off the heat. All the juices will flow into the plate and you'll have a dry tasting steak.

HOW TO TELL IF YOUR STEAK IS COOKED THE WAY YOU LIKE

Most people like their steaks cooked rare, medium rare, or medium. The more you cook steaks, the better you'll get at telling when a steak is done to your liking. Never, ever, cut into a steak checking for doneness.

Instead, poke the steak with your index finger before you begin cooking. Sense how raw feels. Then poke the fleshy part of your palm, right below your thumb, with your hand relaxed. You'll find that it feels much like the raw, or rare, steak feels. Now tighten your hand slowly, while still poking that fleshy part of the palm. As you close your hand, the fleshy part of your palm will become firmer, the way meat does as it cooks. When your grip is closed, your palm will feel as meat does when it is well done. Very quickly you'll be able to gauge the way various stages of doneness feels just by touching meat. The firmer it feels, the more done your steak is. It's that simple.

Against the grain, slice the steak into ¼-inch slices, and let it remain in the buttery garlic juices until you are ready to eat. You'll go crazy, it tastes so good. Serve with Buttermilk Vidalia Onion Rings (page 103).

HAMBURGERS TO DIE FOR

All hamburger meat should be salted, then mixed, before cooking.

1 pound ground sirloin, salted
2 tablespoons cold butter

Toppings for the Best Burger

Mayonnaise on both sides of buttered grilled bun
Dijon Mustard on top of burger
2 slices American or cheddar cheeses or 2 ounces blue cheese, melted
5 slices cooked bacon
Sautéed onions
Sautéed mushrooms

To each ½-pound burger patty, add one tablespoon of ice cold butter in the middle, making sure the butter is completely on the inside of the burger and covered by the meat. Fry or grill as preferred. It will make the best tasting burger you will ever eat.

As while cooking the steak, never cut, flatten, or pierce the burger—the juices will escape, and the meat will be dry to the taste. Always flip with a spatula or tongs. Always butter and grill (or toast) the bun. Never eat a hamburger with a cold bun. Try to refrain from using lettuce or tomato on your burger. Top your burger instead with mayonnaise, mustard, cheese, bacon, sautéed onion, and sautéed mushrooms. And dunk each bite of burger in Heinz ketchup. Serve with lots of homemade french fries.

Makes 1 incredible burger

Note: Many think that salting beef will only make the meat tough—but if you salt the beef only right before cooking, it will have no time to draw out the natural juices.

"Pack on the Pounds"
on Your Next Family Vacation

TAKE A CRUISE

NEXT TO THE BUFFET TABLES IN LAS VEGAS, NOTHING BEATS TAKING A LUXURIOUS CRUISE FOR PACKING ON THE POUNDS. Think about it; you can literally eat all day and all night on most cruise ships. Forget about the ports of call. Who cares where the ship sails to—tell your friendly travel agent that you are looking for the best food cruise line in the business, even if it sails only to Pascagoula, Mississippi, and back.

When asked if you want first or second seating, tell them you want both. Wake up early for the breakfast buffet, and make sure you attend the mid-morning snack table, and all mid-afternoon teas, while you lounge poolside waiting for the first and second seating at dinner. Remember you can also order room service.

After dinner, go watch an in-board movie while they set up the midnight buffet. It's best if you get in line by 11:00 P.M. so you can be there ahead of anyone else, and while the food is hot and tasty. Remember to always use your scooter to get around the ship to avoid burning too many calories.

BEST DARN MEATLOAF IN AMERICA

As we were growing up, my mom would fix our favorite meals for our birthdays, and my favorite meal was meatloaf, mashed potatoes, and peas. To this day, for me it's one of the best meals anyone can serve. This meatloaf is like none I've ever had anywhere. Using Ritz crackers for the inside and topping it with thinly sliced onion, bacon, and canned concentrated Campbell's tomato soup makes it one of the most moist yet firm meatloaves you will ever taste.

¼ cup (½ stick) butter

8 garlic cloves, finely chopped or pressed

2 medium onions, chopped

4 ¼ pounds ground beef, chuck, round—it's up to you

3 tablespoons Worcestershire sauce

3 tablespoons Dijon mustard

5 heaping tablespoons ketchup

1 teaspoon salt

2 eggs

2 packages (tubes) Ritz crackers, crushed with your hands

1 cup or 1 bundle fresh Italian parsley

1 teaspoon pepper

4 cans of Campbell's tomato soup

Heat the butter in a skillet and sauté the garlic and onions until tender. In a large mixing bowl, add the ground chuck, Worcestershire sauce, Dijon mustard, ketchup, salt, eggs, crackers, Italian parsley, pepper, and sautéed onion and garlic mixture. Mix together well.

Preheat oven to 350 degrees. Form mixture into the size meatloaf you desire. Never use a loaf pan. Your meatloaf should be free-formed in a large baking pan. Each meatloaf should be topped with thinly sliced onion, and bacon slices. It can be frozen at this stage. Bake for 20 minutes—pour the Campbell's tomato soup over the top and continue to bake until done, about another 30 minutes. If you are making the entire 4¼ pounds of meat, you will need 6 to 8 cans of soup, but at least 4 cans per meatloaf. The more the better. It makes a great sauce.

Makes 5 servings

ITALIAN MEATBALLS

Another one of my favorite meals is spaghetti and meatballs. People usually don't add enough flavor to the meat, but you will find that these have tremendous flavor. (You've probably guessed by now that my favorite meal is the one I'm currently eating.)

    1 Best Darned Meatloaf (page 108), uncooked
    1 cup freshly grated Parmesan or Romano cheese
    1 green pepper, finely chopped
    2 tablespoons dried oregano
    2 tablespoons dried basil
    1 teaspoon red pepper flakes

To the meatloaf recipe, add the Parmesan or Romano cheese. Add the green pepper to the onion-garlic mixture and sauté. Add the oregano, basil, and red pepper at the end with the other spices in the meatloaf recipe. Form into large balls. Cook the meatballs in a little homemade marinara sauce (page 110). You just need to barely cover the meatballs, and it will take 6 to 8 cups of sauce for about 60 meatballs. You could even use a high quality bottled sauce such as Paul Newman's. Once done, remove the meatballs from the sauce and put them in homemade sauce. Meatballs are good on top of spaghetti all covered with cheese, or in a hoagie roll all covered with cheese, or on top of an extra large pizza . . . you guessed it—all covered with cheese.

Makes about 60 meatballs (enough for 2)

Note: Use the sauce to flavor the meatballs but never meatballs to flavor your sauce. Cooking the raw meatballs in a sauce enhances the flavor of the meatballs, but don't use the sauce the meatballs are cooked in—discard it, because it has now been flavored by the meatballs. Most people either bake or fry their meatballs and then put them in the sauce. You don't want to add the meatballs to the entire sauce until cooked, because it will change the flavor of your primary sauce.

INCREDIBLE MARINARA SAUCE

Everyone has a favorite spaghetti sauce—and this is mine. I've been making it for years. This sauce can be used for all sorts of things. You can, of course, serve it over spaghetti. But you can also pour one-fourth cup over crispy fried chicken breast with melted mozzarella and Parmesan on top for the best tasting chicken Parmesans you'll ever sink your teeth into.

3 carrots, finely chopped	6 small cans tomato paste
6 celery stalks, chopped	¼ cup Lea & Perrins
3 large onions, chopped	Worcestershire sauce
2 medium green peppers	Salt and pepper to taste (begin
1 cup fresh parsley	with 2 teaspoons salt and
8 large garlic cloves	1 teaspoon pepper)
5 tablespoons dried oregano	1 teaspoon red pepper flakes
5 tablespoons dried basil	½ cup extra-virgin olive oil to
½ cup suga	rbegin sautéing aromatic
2 (1-gallon) cans Hunt's crushed	vegetables
tomatoes	

In a large pot that will hold more than 2 gallons, sauté carrots, celery, onions, green peppers, parsley and garlic in olive oil. Sauté until soft. Add remaining ingredients and simmer on medium-low heat for 3 to 5 hours. Best when made a day ahead.

Variations: Add ½ cup canned kidney beans to 2 cups of sauce and a tablespoon of chili powder, and you have a great tasting vegetarian chili (or you can add ground beef or sausage if you wish).

Try adding ¼ pound of peeled and deveined fresh shrimp in 2 cups of the sauce to make a shrimp Creole. Serve it with ¼ cup cooked white rice or ½ cup cooked penne pasta.

Also, if you add the shrimp and 2 cups of sauce, you will have a super tasting thick and hearty soup—serve it in a bowl and add a tablespoon of freshly grated Parmesan or Romano cheese, served with a salad. You'll never go back to the low-fat or low-calorie stuff!

Chapter Eight

WHEN YOU'RE HOME ALONE

QUICK AND EASY MACARONI AND CHEESE

 1 cup plus ¼ cup butter (2½ sticks)

 1 cup all-purpose flour

 1 quart milk

 1 quart half-and-half (maybe more)

 ½ teaspoon salt (more if desired)

 ½ teaspoon pepper (more if desired)

 3 pounds American cheese (get an unsliced block and grate yourself)

 2 pounds elbow macaroni, boiled in salted water and drained

Melt the 1 cup butter in large saucepan. Add flour and make a light brown roux by cooking for about 10 minutes over medium–high heat, stirring constantly. Add milk and half-and-half, 1 cup at a time. (You may need to add as much as 2 or 3 more cups.) Keep on medium–high heat, stirring constantly until relatively thick. Then add salt, pepper, remaining ¼ cup butter, and grated cheese. Stir until a nice cheese sauce is created. Taste and add more of whatever you may like. Preheat the oven to 350 degrees.

Mix with the cooked and drained macaroni, top with grated American cheese, and bake until a nice brown crust forms on the top and it is very hot and bubbly, about 30 to 45 minutes.

Makes 1 serving

REALLY GOOD AND REALLY EASY HOMEMADE CHICKEN POT PIE

This recipe is so easy, you'll keep making it over and over, and loving every single bite. You can use any frozen vegetable you like. And, yes, we realize that there are vegetables in this dish; however, we think there is enough butter and flour to more than compensate for the few calories in the veggies.

1 large roasted chicken from grocery (or 2 small ones)
8 regular size cans chicken stock
1 (12 to 16-ounce) package frozen black-eyed peas
1 (12 to 16-ounce) package frozen baby lima beans
1 (10-ounce) small bag baby carrots
1 (12 to 16-ounce) package frozen peas
1 (12 to 16-ounce) package frozen corn
1 (12 to 16-ounce) package frozen pearl onions
1 cup (2 sticks) salted butter
1 cup all-purpose flour
3 packages Jiffy corn muffin mix
3 eggs for corn muffin mix
1 cup milk for corn muffin mix
  Salt and black pepper

Take the chicken off the bone and remove the skin. Cut into small bite-size pieces. Do not throw away the cooked and spicy skin—this you can enjoy while cooking the pot pie.

In a heavy-bottomed large pot, bring the chicken stock to a boil. Add the black-eyed peas, bring to a boil, and cook for 15 minutes, then add the limas. Bring the chicken stock back to a boil and cook for 5 minutes. Add the carrots and boil for 5 minutes. Add the peas, corn, and onions and boil for a full 5 minutes. When the vegetables are cooked, strain through a colander or strainer, reserving the stock.

Melt the butter in the empty pot. Add the flour and whisk constantly on medium-high to high heat for about 5 minutes. Now add the chicken stock and the vegetables, about 2 cups at a time until all the stock is added, making a rich thick gravy-like consistency. Add salt and black pepper to taste, and add the vegetables and chicken to pot. Preheat the oven to 375 degrees.

Pour into multiple (or one large) buttered casserole(s). Make the Jiffy corn muffins according to the package directions and spoon over the top of the chicken pot pie(s), covering the entire casserole. Bake until the topping is cooked, brown, and the filling is bubbly, about 30 to 45 minutes. With a knife, check the middle of the cornbread topping to make sure it is cooked on the bottom. If the top is browning too quickly, lightly cover with a piece of aluminum foil.

Makes 1 or 2 pies (2 servings)

Crust Topping Variations
- Store-bought pie pastry (roll it out and place on top)
- Any high quality canned biscuit (flaky is very good)
- Any high quality uncooked frozen biscuit (just put on top frozen and bake)

COGNAC-BRAISED SHORT RIBS

My Auntie Louise "Weesy" would make us the best short ribs when we visited her in Bedford, Massachusetts. You will love the taste of these slow-cooked short ribs. Believe it or not, short ribs are expensive, especially because you need so many to make a meal—plus adding a fine cognac to this delectable dish makes it a bit on the pricey side. Yet it's well worth it for a special occasion.

Salt and pepper	4 bay leaves
10 pounds short ribs (with bone)	4 sprigs rosemary
Flour for dredging ribs	4 large garlic cloves
1 stick butter (more as needed)	1 cup tomato paste
½ cup vegetable oil (more as needed)	3 tablespoons Lea & Perrins Worcestershire sauce
6 slices bacon, chopped	
5 large carrots, chopped	4 tablespoons sugar
2 large white onions, chopped	2 cups fine cognac
2 celery stalks	(we recommend Hennessy)
1 (32-ounce) can chopped tomatoes	

Rub salt and pepper into all the short ribs and dredge them in flour, shaking off excess flour. In a large heavy-bottomed pot, melt 1 stick of the butter and the oil until the mixture is smoking hot. Carefully put one layer of short ribs in hot oil and let them develop a solid crust (this is called braising or caramelizing). Braise on all sides and remove from the pot. Keep adding butter and oil as needed for braising. Continue until all the ribs are braised.

In the pot with all the juices from the braising, throw in bacon pieces and onion, and cook until onions are soft. Really scrape the bottom of the pot as you stir, for you want all those cooked flavors. Add all the remaining ingredients and bring to a hard boil. Add the short ribs, and cook on medium-low heat for about 4 hours or in a 350-degree oven (if you have an ovenproof pot) for the same amount of time—or until the ribs are fall-off-the-bone tender. If cooking on top of the stove, make sure you scrape and stir the bottom of pot so it doesn't burn. Add canned beef stock or cognac if more liquid is needed. The short ribs should be barely covered.

You may serve them now, but we recommend that you let the short ribs cool in the pot and gravy, then reheat. It will intensify the flavors tremendously, and it's even better if cooked the day before.

Serve with mashed potatoes made with butter and cream or white rice.

Makes 4 servings

Note: Be *very* careful not to drop the ribs back in the hot oil, for it can sear the skin off your hands.

AUTHENTIC SWISS FONDUE

Fondues were part of the 1970s culture, but in our house fondues never left. Nothing packs on the pounds better than lots of pieces of bread dunked in warm rich cheese sauce. This fondue recipe is the best I've found, from Chef Marty Blitz of the Mise En Place restaurant in Tampa, Florida.

    1 garlic clove
    2 French bread baguettes
    3 tablespoons white flour
    ½ pound Gruyère cheese, grated
    ½ pound Emmenthaler cheese, grated
    ½ pound Appenzeller cheese, grated
    2 cups dry Chardonnay (no other wine is acceptable)
    ¼ cup port wine
      Pinch of nutmeg

Slice the garlic once and rub the inside of your fondue pot. Slice the baguettes into bite-size pieces and keep covered. Mix the flour evenly into the grated cheese. Heat the Chardonnay over medium heat until just before a boil. Add the cheese, stirring constantly and slowly. Once melted, add the port and immediately pour into the fondue pot. Sprinkle the nutmeg on top. Keep fondue warm in fondue pot with chafing dish fuel. Using long fondue forks, dunk the chucks of French bread into the fondue. Indulge yourself!

Makes 1 midnight snack or 2 lunch servings

PULLED PORK BUTT SO GOOD, YOU'LL WANNA KICK YOURSELF

"Pork fat rules!" So says incredible chef and Food Network guru and restaurant owner Emeril Lagasse. We believe Emeril when he says *pork fat rules* . . . a credo to live by. This easy pork recipe will delight your friends and family to no end. And it's so easy too!

       Salt and pepper
    2 very large (about 6 pounds each) pork butts (commonly called pork
       shoulders or Boston butts)
   40 garlic cloves (you can buy it already peeled, but fresh is best—never use
       pre-chopped)
   10 bay leaves

Preheat the oven to 250 degrees. Liberally salt and pepper pork butts. Do not trim fat from your butts. Put half of the garlic on the bottom of a large pan, then the butts, then the remaining garlic and bay leaves. Cover tightly with two sheets of aluminum foil to make sure no air escapes.

Bake for 12 hours. Let cool and pull apart using two forks. This butt needs no sauces; just let it sit in its own juices after it's pulled. The juices are awesome over white rice. If you must have an additional sauce, this is great served with homemade or your favorite bottled barbecue sauce inside a fresh hoagie roll. Great for having friends over to watch games on television, but you might want to double the recipe.

Makes 6 servings

Variation: Cuban-Style Pulled Pork Butt. Keep all the ingredients above and add 8 tablespoons dried oregano, 3 cups sour orange juice (comes in a bottle at specialty markets and some grocery stores—it's not typical OJ), 3 cups Mojo (also comes in a bottle, usually found in Latin or Cuban markets). Follow the directions for the pork butt. After the butt is salted and peppered, rub each butt with 4 tablespoons of dried oregano. Pour sour orange juice and Mojo over butts and follow the cooking directions above. Great served with black beans and white or yellow rice. And don't forget the fried plantains.

GOURMET FLAVOR ENHANCERS

In addition to the most recommended flavor enhancers such as butter, sour cream, and mayonnaise, which go great on everything, we suggest venturing forth to new culinary heights and trying the following.

Caramelized Onion Relish

Melt 1 stick of butter in skillet. Thinly slice 6 large Vidalia onions. Add ½ cup sugar and ¼ cup balsamic vinegar, and sauté very slowly over medium to medium-low heat until the onions are caramelized deep brown (not burned). This can take an hour or longer, but is really worth your time. Use as a sandwich condiment or topping for fried anything.

The Ultimate Fried Anything

Double coat everything you eat: chicken, beef, pork, shrimp, fish, and even those low-cal vegetables such as mushrooms, zucchini, and green tomatoes. Coat food in seasoned flour (shake off excess), dip in beaten eggs and milk mixture, then back in the seasoned flour, then again in the egg-milk mixture, and then finally in seasoned bread crumbs. There will be a solid inch of fried coating all around your food. (We got this idea from a master chef to the overweight stars, who prefers to remain anonymous.)

Salt: Our Favorite Flavor Enhancer

Excessive use of salt is a great way to help put on extra pounds when you are having difficulty adding weight, or feeling a bit light overall. The more salt you use, the better. It will help retain water and actually make you look heavier than you really are, especially in your ankles.

EASY SLOW-COOKED BRISKET POT ROAST

This slow–cooked brisket is the best tasting piece of meat you'll ever enjoy cooking. And the best thing is that you will spend less than fifteen minutes in preparation time.

   Salt and pepper
 2 very large beef briskets (with fat on)
 6 large carrots, peeled and chopped into 3-inch pieces
 2 large white onions, peeled and roughly chopped
 4 celery stalks, chopped
 2 sprigs fresh rosemary
24 garlic cloves (yes, you heard us right, 24 cloves), crushed
 1 cup tomato paste

Preheat the oven to 250 degrees. Liberally salt and pepper the briskets on both sides, leaving the fat on the brisket. In an ovenproof large casserole pot with cover or a large baking pan (which you will tightly cover with aluminum foil), place half of the ingredients in the pan, lay the briskets on top, then throw in the remaining ingredients.

Cover tightly with aluminum foil and then the lid. Bake for 9 to 12 hours. Put it in the oven by 8 P.M. and take it out before you go to work the next morning. It's that easy. Let cool before slicing. Serve with mashed potatoes or rice, or both.

Makes 2 servings

PART III
LIVING THE NORTH BEACH WAY

Chapter Nine

EVERYDAY LIFE ON THE NORTH BEACH DIET

Always go grocery shopping when you are starving—right after a hard day's work is usually a great time. Never take a list, for impulse buying is best. If on a budget, remember that Little Debbie Snack Cakes are an affordable buy, and can make a super dinner all by themselves.

After an especially tough day at the office, you might not feel like shopping. Plan for those days in advance; and make a quick dash by the store to pick up several large baked potatoes (served loaded with bacon, butter, and sour cream) plus a box of Little Debbie Devil Crème Snack Cakes. It's a quick meal, and just what the doctor ordered to sooth the tensions of the day.

Life with the Kids

Encourage your children to lie around the house as much as possible, eating and watching television or using their Play Station. There is no better bonding experience for the whole family. Also teaching your children how to bake cookies, cakes, and pies will be a calming influence for those kids who are a bit rambunctious.

Your Sex Life

Your sex life will be greatly enhanced while on The North Beach Diet. You will find that there is no better time to enjoy sex with your

OUR QUALITY PROGRAMMING PICKS

While we prefer you watch only the Food Network, at least the first month on our plan, there are a few television shows on major networks worth viewing. Check your local listings for days and times.

220/220 (ABC)

Barbara Walters returns to evening news programming at a hefty 220 pounds. B. Walters does it again, bringing Katie Couric to tears, as she discusses in this "exclusive" primetime interview the dilemmas of being thin in an industry catering to the plus-size woman. Compelling and insightful!

Dr. Fat 90210 (MTV)

This reality-based show follows Beverly Hills Pharmacology students on their quest to develop a pill to increase weight without eating. Why anyone would want to gain weight without eating is beyond us—but who knows about kids these days?

The Chubby Apprentice (NBC)

Donald Trump loses his hair (thankfully), gains weight, and brings together the "Biggest and the Brightest" young adults Wharton, Kellogg, and Harvard Business School has to offer. The premiere episode highlights their first task of creating a new cake mix and frosting for Duncan Hines with over 1,800 calories a slice.

OTHER NOTABLE MENTIONS

CSI-McDonald's (CBS)

Fat Bachelor Meets Extreme Cuisine (FOX)

Tele-Tubby-Tubbies (PBS)

Flaw & Order (NBC) Sundays, After *All My Fat Children,* starring Erika Sugar-Kane. First episode deals with hate-crimes against thin village people.

spouse than after a hearty meal, on a full stomach. Pulled Pork Butt (page 116) and your favorite baked beans should be eaten as a prelude to sex.

Recently, a quadruple non-sighted study was conducted by the head test-kitchen cook at the University Culinary Institute of Colorado. Holly Barber, who holds a prestigious AA Degree in Digestive Juices, found that most children in the United States were born in the months of August and September, basically nine months after the Thanksgiving and Christmas holiday eating period.

- *Best Outdoor Activities for Weight Gain:* Club seats at a professional ball stadium, picnics, floating on a large raft in a large pool
- *Best Indoor Activities for Weight Gain:* Watching television while relaxing in your La-Z-Boy recliner

Indulge Your Children's Food Consumption: They Know Best

"Okay, okay, get real," you may be saying. "I've got a two-year-old whose entire reason for living is to make our time at dinner miserable. As soon as we get to the table he begins yelling and throwing food. It's not conducive to anything, much less having an enjoyable mealtime." If this is your experience, try the North Beach Diet plan for kids. We recommend feeding little Johnny whenever and whatever he wants. Think of how many fights you'll save if you give him a box of chocolate cream-filled Ho Ho's for dinner. If your child demands Skittles and M&Ms for breakfast—provide all she can eat.

It's good to have your children participate in grocery shopping at an early age as well. Most parents hate the thought of taking their kids to a grocery. But think through the reasons. Parents at the grocery store are constantly telling their child *no* to everything they want. Dr. Stephen White, PhD, noted family therapist, best-selling author, White House Fellow, and president of Douglas Pharmaceuticals housed in the laboratories at the University of Dijon in Dijon, France, said it best: "Our vast studies have shown that when parents indulge their child's every whim, in every way possible, denying them nothing, it reduces the overall tension within the family household by a staggering 78.9 percent and allowing for a freedom of expression far beyond the typical child."

Our point will be proved the first trip to the grocery. When they ask for it—they get it. Chips? Sure. Oreos? Of course, darling. Three boxes of Lucky Charms? No problem. They ask for it, it's theirs ... without a hint of negativity from Mommy and Daddy. And the dinner table should be just the same. If you've prepared a fine dinner of steak, loaded baked potatoes, and pecan pie, and they want pasta—give it to them. Just think how calm and stress-free your life will be, thus allowing you to better follow your new plan for fast weight gain.

> **For happy kids, encourage them to spend hours watching TV. What channel, you may ask? The Food Network! Is there any other network?**

Las Vegas Buffets: The Vacation Spot for the Entire Family

Vacations are a necessary part of life's little rejuvenation process. And there is no better place to vacation while on the North Beach Diet plan than good ole Las Vegas.

Skip the one-arm bandits and the crap tables and spend your time eating your way though the "All You Can Eat" Buffet Capital of the world. You and your family will bond like never before by seeing who can pile their plates higher at the Palladium Buffet.

A fun "Who Can Eat the Most Eggs Benedict and Waffles" contest at the Golden Nugget Breakfast Buffet will surely catapult you to the "Feast Around the World Buffet" for lunch at the Green Valley Ranch. And what could be more fun for the kids than a wholesome midnight dessert-eating competition at the French Market Buffet?

Not only will the entire family have oodles of fun, you'll be teaching them the basics of consuming mass quantities of high-calorie food five times a day. One day they too will be able to pass on these same techniques to their children. Now *those* are family values.

The Best Las Vegas Buffets

(Warning: Do not tell them you are on the North Beach Diet Plan, or they will turn you away.)

Big Kitchen, The
Bally's Las Vegas
3645 Las Vegas Blvd.
(702) 967-4930

Buffet at Bellagio, The
Bellagio
3600 Las Vegas Blvd.
(702) 693-8111

Carnival World Buffet
Rio All-Suite Hotel & Casino
3700 West Flamingo Rd.
(702) 252-7777

French Market Buffet
Palm's Casino Resort
4321 West Flamingo Rd.
(866) 942-7777

Feast around the World
Green Valley Ranch
2300 Pasco Verde Pkwy.
Henderson, NV
(702) 617-7777

Le Village Buffet Golden
Nugget Buffet
Golden Nugget Hotel & Casino
129 East Fremont St.
(702) 385-7111

Village Buffet Paladium
Caesar's Palace
3570 Las Vegas Blvd.
(702) 731-7731

Village Seafood Buffet
Rio All-Suite Hotel & Casino
3700 West Flamingo Rd.
(702) 252-7777

"I AM A FAT AMERICAN"

Recently, the governor of the garden state of Hawaii was caught in a scandal of epicurean proportions. While at the same time he was accepting bids from the Wendy's Restaurant chain to place fast food establishments in all pre-school, elementary, and secondary schools throughout the state, he was found partying and accepting Golden Arches from his new-found friend, Australian Attaché for Gastronomic Affairs, Lt. Col. Ron McDonald.

While both McDonald and Governor Jim McFeely denied any wrongdoing, the governor thought it best if he resigned from office, allowing him to spend "more time eating with his family."

Regardless of the scandal, every overweight person in the United States can be proud—for when the governor finally came out of the pantry, he bravely declared himself a Fat American.

Fast Food : A Primary Source to a Whole New You

Fast food establishments have taken a hit in recent years, and rightly so. They have left their roots and have begun offering a lighter fare, even eliminating the super-sized menu in many places, and including a wide variety of salads. Admittedly we are concerned.

We were happy to hear that a "watch-dog" group has been formed to oversee the standards and practices of the fast food industry. Food And Truth (FAT) has gotten off to a quick start, reviewing the most commonly heard complaints from its overweight patrons. The top four complaints about fast food restaurants are:

1) Not enough fat is used in cooking.
2) Beef lard is no longer used for frying.
3) The super-sized offerings remain too small.
4) Salads, salads, salads—okay, already, enough with the salads; this is a fast food establishment! We want hamburgers, french fries, milk shakes, tacos, fried chicken! Do what you do best, and let someone else do the rest—get back to your roots!

Food And Truth (FAT) has assured us that it will sue if necessary to restore the fat in these products. You may contribute to the FAT campaign through us at www.northbeachdietonline.com. Fast food restaurants are very good for you, but some need a gentle push to stay on the fat-track.

For your benefit, we have provided the following helpful tips to maximize your caloric intake.

Smart Tips to Maximize Fast Food Enjoyment

McDonald's

Even though we were sorely disappointed that McDonald's succumbed to the food police, changing the frying oil from lard to canola oil—most of us still think that McDonald's has the best french fries of all the fast food establishments. Our tip is to order a small fry, smash the entire pack between a Quarter Pounder with Cheese, and enjoy. Note: This small fry does not take the place of a large pack, which you should consume as well.

Burger King

Burger King is the place to have it your way for breakfast. What can be better for you than deep fried battered bread sticks with rich maple syrup? Because it only provides five French Toast Sticks per order, we recommend a minimum of five orders per person at any given breakfast—and make sure you request a minimum of two maple syrups per order.

Wendy's

The Wendy's Chocolate Frosty is awesome. Our tip is to order two large Frostys and save one in your freezer to drink with your breakfast instead of juice. Since Wendy's does not open for breakfast, this is a good alternative.

Kentucky Fried Chicken (KFC)

Even though KFC is one of the North Beach Diet's favorite places, we were close to denying them listing status in our program. They are trying to mask the word *fried* by using only initials, denying the true benefits of deep fat frying. Our tip is to always order Extra-Crispy.

Taco Bell

We are very proud of Taco Bell for not caving in to the food police—even its salads are covered with beef, re-fried beans, and cheese. While we have no one particular tip, we highly recommend extra cheese and extra sour cream on everything.

Subway

We cannot recommend Subway. Jared, come back to us? We'll help you.

Oprah, Where Have You Gone, Girl?

Celebrity Failures

Does everyone succeed on the North Beach Diet? Sadly, no. We have had some celerity notables who have been challenged with our program.

We had such high hopes for Oprah Winfrey, for example—but she made the wrong connection by befriending our arch-nemeses Dr. Phil and Bob Greene. Now, after years of hope, unfortunately, Oprah has been added to our top ten celebrity failures.

While we do not like to single people out, we provide the following list as an encouragement, letting you know that yes, even celebrities can have difficulty maintaining a hefty weight. If you ever see them on the street—don't mock and jeer their thinness—say a little prayer for them, for only by the grace of God go I.

The Top Ten Celebrity Weight Gain Failures

1. The entire staff at *Vogue* magazine
2. Sarah Ferguson (Duchess of York)
3. Oprah Winfrey
4. Carnie Wilson
5. Whoopi Goldberg
6. Anna Nicole Smith
7. Starr Jones
8. Al Roker
9. Jamie Atkinson
10. Former President Bill Clinton*

A Serious Note about Bill Clinton

In the fall of 2004, former President Bill Clinton underwent quadruple heart bypass surgery in New York City. While we empathize with his health plight, we predicted that it would not be long before this happened. You see, Mr. Clinton quit eating fast food, began to exercise, and lost weight. Some saw him as fit—we realized however, it was only a matter of time before he would keel over. We should all take this as a warning—*Do Not Abandon* the North Beach Diet program!

INTELLECTUAL FUN FOR THE WHOLE FAMILY

Find a map of the world—pick a region, and figure out how many food names or food sayings you can make up using a particular country or city. For example, using Middle Eastern countries, we have

- **Turkey:** Turkey and Dressing
- **Tunisia:** Tunisia on Rye
- **Yemen:** Yemen Meringue Pie
- **Strait of Hormusz:** Strait of Humus with Falafel
- **Gaza Strip:** Gaza Strip Steak and Potatoes
- **Oman:** Oman, this is good pie!

Bloviate and Opine At Every Opportunity

Bloviate: To orate on and on, never stop talking
Opine: To rant, preach, harangue

While on the North Beach Diet, never let an opportunity go by without endlessly talking about the success you are having on your new lifestyle change. Whether on a subway or elevator, at a lunch counter or fine restaurant, ballpark, or museum, you should constantly be looking for ways to interject the great results you are having on this program.

When you see someone eating lean turkey, fruits, and vegetables, look for ways to espouse your eating prowess. Maybe a comment such as "You wouldn't be so thin if you joined my program," or "Have you ever thought about combining that turkey with some Wonder Bread, Hellman's mayonnaise, Kraft American cheese food product, and Oscar Mayer maple-cured bacon?"

And don't forget to compliment them with comments such as, "You have such a pretty face—if you only gained fifty or sixty pounds, you'd be perfect."

New York Times columnist William O. Reilly, internationally acclaimed orator, holding the prestigious A. L. Frankin chair from the Institute of the Criminally Insane, himself a fat American who is always looking out for us, recommends that you never be pithy while discussing your weight gain. He writes: "Never miss an opportunity to tell someone how they should live their lives."

JOIN THE EFFORT TO BUILD A MONUMENT HONORING THE BRAVE FAT AMERICAN SOLDIER

Roosevelt, Jefferson, Lincoln, Washington, World War II veterans, Vietnam veterans, and nurses are all honored with monuments and statues in our great capital in Washington, D.C. Yet there is one group left out: The Brave Fat American Soldier. This is a travesty of justice.

We are proposing that the Congress of The United States provide immediate funding for a monument commemorating the heroism of the many great Fat Americans who gave their lives protecting us against the over-taxation of food products. The monument should be entitled "A Band of Fat Brothers."

You too can play an integral role in this weighty endeavor by sending a postcard to your Congressman, Congresswoman, and Senator right this very moment. Don't delay. Also, donations can be made to help offset the expenses of this effort, with checks payable to:

The Center for Fat American Justice
Post Office Box 14304
Tampa, Florida 33629

For Further Information Contact Our Website:
www.northbeachdietonline.com

Chapter Ten

VIRTUAL EXERCISE: GOOD FOR MIND AND BODY

Stay in Shape with Our "Body-By-Cake" Program

- Pie-laties
- NordicSnack
- Capt'n Crunches

A Word of Caution

If you ever, ever, experience light-headedness, dizziness, an inability to lift a fork, shortness of breath, or muscle strain of any kind during virtual exercise—STOP IMMEDIATELY! Turn off the video or CD player, and begin to consume one normal-sized box of Cheese Nips washed down with an orange soda—any brand will do. If symptoms continue, visit your local Baskin-Robbins for further treatment before continuing. In fact, we recommend you visit Baskin-Robbins before starting. An ounce of prevention is worth a pound of cure.

Virtual Exercise

Think about it . . . no more walking, jogging, swimming, biking, hiking, aerobic dancing—no exercise of any kind. All you have to do on our program is sit and eat. And the added advantage with our Virtual Exercise program: You don't have to check with your doctor before you begin.

You Gotta Sit!

The most significant reason for your success with the North Beach Diet program will be your ability to take control, first of your eating and then of your non-activity level. Becoming non-active does two things. First, you don't burn excess calories (or lower your metabolism) and second, it makes you feel good. Both of these will contribute to your overall success.

Most exercise increases your metabolism; this is not good for long-term success on our program. Everyone knows that effective weight gain is nothing more than lowering metabolism—without burning calories. Our virtual exercise program will lower your metabolism for up to sixteen hours. What more could you ask for?

It is always best to sit in a comfortable La-Z-Boy recliner while performing our patented Virtual Exercise programs.

Eat First

Before you begin virtual exercise, eat a little something. The perfect pre-exercise breakfast is two soft-fried eggs, hash browns, cream of wheat or grits, four slices of Texas Cheese Toast with Smucker's Strawberry Preserves, chocolate milk, and a slice of cool refreshing cantaloupe (I know, I know, the cantaloupe is cheating, but it tastes so good).

Do you think Lance Armstrong would ever begin a day on the grueling Tour de France without eating first? Of course not. And you shouldn't begin your day without eating either.

Remember too, you should hydrate yourself with mass quantities of 7-Up or Coca-Cola while exercising. It's important to stay hydrated throughout the process. Note: No diet sodas allowed.

Slower Is Always Better

The North Beach goal is to slow your metabolism to a snail's pace. Hence the slower you move, the better to reach optimum results with our program. Begin gradually and move as little as possible. The first week we want you to rest at least twenty minutes after all meals are consumed. Each week thereafter, add five minutes of rest to your routine until you reach an hour of total relaxation after each meal.

Tips to Lower Metabolism

- We highly suggest that you purchase a riding Mobility Cart for easy moving around the house, neighborhood, office, and grocery stores. We recommend the Pacesaver – Passport III model, which can be purchased directly from Planet Mobility's website at www.planetmobility.com. It's the best investment you'll ever make.
- Immediately secure a handicapped sticker for your car.
- Park as close to the entrance to all buildings as possible.
- Always use handicap mobility carts. If one is not available at the store where you shop—contact a local law firm and sue!

Our Patented Program Designed for the Young at Heart

Call your local video store, and say you want the North Beach Diet Virtual Exercise Series—The Starter Pack. This comes with these following videos or DVDs that feature a fitness theme:

- *Chariots of Fire*
- *Rocky*
- *Rocky II* (Note: The remaining Rocky movies are part of our advanced program.)
- *Jane Fonda's Aerobic Workout* (This is an oldie, but a goodie; just be careful to resist the urge to exercise along with Jane.)
- *Rudy*

The series also comes with

- A six-pack of Coca-Cola
- 3 packs of Skittles
- 4 packs of Sno-Caps
- 2 Butterfingers
- 4 packs of Milky Way Bites
- 3 large bags of Lay's sour cream and onion potato chips
- 1 bag of Doritos
- 2 packs of Slim Jims

Make sure you indicate whether you want videos or DVDs, and to ask the store to deliver all the items to you—it's important not to exert yourself too much by going directly to the store. Sadly, most video stores have yet to invest in the mini Mobility Riding Carts that many grocery stores offer to their patrons.

We have negotiated a 10 percent discount on the first order, at participating video stores.

Cardio-Intervals

Hot tubs are perfect for Cardio-Intervals. Begin by sitting in your hot tub, fifteen minutes to start, then increasing your time each week until you reach an hour.

Always—yes, we mean always—bring refreshments into the tub while doing Cardio-Intervals. We suggest beer or high-fructose soft drinks—but no glass bottles, please. Safety first! We also recommend extra salty pretzels and chips, to replace any salt loss from the heat of the tub water.

Keep your breathing cadence slow and easy. Breathe with your diaphragm by extending and relaxing your abdominals. Feel your belly. Take in the experience. Meditate on your favorite food. Focus on your relaxation.

The Dangers of Strength Training and Aerobic Exercise

Increasing your muscle mass will raise your metabolism and allow you to burn fat instead of storing it. This is a no-no on our program. The key is to lower your metabolism to the lowest possible rate. A regular aerobic walking program and strength training regime is probably the most dangerous way to prevent the increase of adipose tissue (fat).

Aerobic exercise is any activity that can be sustained at a consistent pace and allows you to talk comfortably, such as walking, aerobic dancing, NordicTrack, jogging, rowing, stair climbing, or indoor or outdoor biking. We have found that constant walking is certainly one of the worst detriments to significant weight gain, which is why we highly recommend the Scooter Mobile for all forms of transportation while on our program.

Below is a chart outlining exactly how many calories you will needlessly burn by walking.

Calories Burned Each Minute of Walking

SPEED (MPH)

	2	2.5	3	3.5	4	4.5	5	6
WEIGHT (LBS)								
110	2.1	2.4	2.8	3.1	4.1	5.2	6.8	9.2
120	2.3	2.6	3.0	3.4	4.4	5.6	7.2	10.1
130	2.5	2.9	3.2	3.6	4.6	6.1	7.8	11.0
140	2.7	3.1	3.5	3.9	5.2	6.6	8.4	11.9
150	2.8	3.3	3.7	4.2	5.6	7.0	9.0	12.8
160	3.0	3.5	4.0	4.5	5.9	7.5	9.6	13.7
170	3.2	3.7	4.2	4.8	6.3	8.0	10.2	14.8
180	3.4	4.0	4.5	5.0	6.7	8.4	10.8	15.5
190	3.6	4.2	4.7	5.3	7.0	8.9	11.4	16.4
200	3.8	4.4	5.0	5.6	7.4	9.4	12.0	17.3
210	4.0	4.6	5.2	5.9	7.8	9.9	12.8	18.2
220	4.2	4.8	5.5	6.2	8.2	10.3	13.2	19.1
230	4.4	5.1	5.7	6.4	8.5	10.8	13.8	20.0
240	4.6	5.3	6.0	6.7	8.9	11.3	14.4	20.9
250	4.8	5.5	6.2	7.0	9.3	11.8	15.0	21.8
260	5.0	5.8	8.5	7.3	9.7	12.2	15.6	22.7
270	5.2	6.0	6.7	7.5	10.0	12.7	16.2	23.6
280	5.4	6.2	7.0	7.8	10.4	13.2	16.8	24.5
290	5.6	6.4	7.2	8.1	10.8	13.6	17.4	25.4
300	5.8	6.7	7.5	8.4	11.2	14.1	18.0	26.3
310	6.0	6.9	7.7	8.7	11.5	14.6	18.6	27.2
320	6.2	7.1	8.0	8.9	11.9	15.1	19.2	28.1
330	6.4	7.4	8.2	9.2	12.3	15.3	19.8	29.0
340	6.6	7.8	8.5	9.5	12.5	16.0	20.4	29.9
350	6.8	8.0	8.7	9.8	12.9	16.5	21.0	30.8

First determine how fast you are walking. You do this by marking off the distance you are walking and keeping track of how long it takes you to complete your walk. Using your new weight each week, refer to the chart to find how many calories you actually are burning each minute. Multiply that number by the total number of minutes you walked. For walking or running, determine your average speed.

For example, if you weigh 200 pounds and you walk a mile in fifteen minutes, you are traveling four miles per hour. Say you walked thirty minutes. Find your weight (200) on the chart and look under 4 mph. Then multiply the thirty minutes you walked by 7.4—you burned 222 calories.

Sounds like you need a Scooter Mobile!

Posturing

It's important to have the right posture while participating in Virtual Exercise. Lying down is always best. And for that we recommend the Panasonic flat screen television attached directly to your ceiling. If you must sit, we highly suggest that you always use the La-Z-Boy recliner. La-Z-Boy makes a super recliner with cup holders and even side storage compartments, so you'll never have to get up and go to the kitchen.

Cookbooks We Recommend

Julia Child

Farewell, Julia: We miss you already!

A delightful, generous spirit and culinary talent passed away in the summer of 2004, Julia Child. She will be sorely missed. We recommend all her cookbooks, but especially these:

Julia Child and Company
Julia Child and More Company
In Julia's Kitchen with Master Chefs
The Way to Cook
Cooking At Home with Julia and Jacques

Martha Stewart

Any book, magazine, or television show Martha Stewart writes and distributes is incredible. She is probably one of the most talented people on earth. Her *Hors D'Ouevres Handbook* is a bible to even the finest chefs, and a must have for your personal library. She is the best of the best, and we can't wait for her new series to begin.

Ina Garten

If you don't know of this lady, you are missing a treat . . . and some good food. Her cookbooks are awesome.

The Barefoot Contessa Cookbook
Barefoot Contessa PARTIES!
Barefoot In Paris

A cookbook by any of the following is a sound investment
• Wolfgang Puck
• Jacques Pepin
• Williams-Sonoma
• James Beard

Best Magazines:
• *Bon Appetit*
• *Gourmet*
• *Southern Living*
• *Cooking Light**

* *Cooking Light* has some very good recipes, just add butter, cream, and salt to every entrée item, and lots more sugar and fat to every dessert item, and you'll be just fine.

Books to Avoid at all Costs:

• Any Richard Simmons product
• *The Ultimate Weight Loss Solution*, by Phillip C. McGraw
• *Eight Days To Optimum Health*, by Andrew Weil
• *The South Beach Diet*, by Arthur Agatston
• Let's just say, all weight loss books

Solid Weight Gain Programs In Addition To the North Beach Diet

We are secure enough in the tenets of our program that we realize that the North Beach Diet may not be the sole answer in your journey to break the cycle of being thin, exercise, and under-eating.

Even if you are on another program, the North Beach Diet is a tremendous complement to that plan, for we've seen nothing better than ours. Here are a few quality programs, none of which limit a food group or pushes drugs. However, I hope that you'll find our program the sole answer. Find what works best for you. Remember too, that the answers ultimately come from you, from within.

• Dr. Atkins—Follow this program for one month straight, then go back eating carbs—you'll be past your desired weight gain in a week . . . guaranteed.

• Peter Lugar's Steak House, Brooklyn—While of course our plan is the best, the Peter Lugar Diet Program is first rate. Use their special Diet Steak Sauce on everything from bread to potatoes—and of course, steak.

• Marie Callender's Frozen Dinner Plan—Fried Chicken, Breaded Pork Chops, Mashed Potatoes with Cream Gravy, you name the food, and it's all allowed on this sensational new program. And her pot pies are super! She provides a complete written plan on her delicious take-home meals.

Chapter Eleven

JOURNALING:
YOUR KEY TO SUCCESS

Hidden within you is a compelling and driving force. Unleash it. Become bold. Dream big dreams. Better yet, dream yourself big. Wake the sleeping giant from within, and make your most audacious visions, dreams, and desires come true.

You are about to discover the finest resources to assist you in your quest to break the cycle of low-fat, low-carb eating. These tools will transform your life, instantly and forever. Let the real you break through.

There are almost as many diets in today's marketplace as there are people. A new one pops up every day, touting the fastest and best way to lose weight, most written by people who have never been big. In my gaining 145 pounds and witnessing countless others who have gained thousands collectively, I can see similarities to our success. I began to understand what worked, and what did not.

I, like most of us, wanted my weight to increase quickly, and I didn't want to work hard either. There was a constant search for the easy way to increase adipose tissue. Since the age of 10, being thin was my way of life. There wasn't a New Year or a birthday that went by that a resolution wasn't made: a commitment to gain weight and be big.

But I had a compulsion to be thin and I'd keep resorting back to countless other programs, countless times: Weight Watchers, Jenny Craig, Physicians Weight Loss, Slim-Fast, Opti-Fast, Atkins, Richard Simmons, Grapefruit, Watermelon, Cabbage, Cambridge, Exlax, amphetamines, self-starvation. You name it and I've probably tried it. Sure, weight increased between these diets, but it usually came right back off, and always faster than it was gained.

If you asked me to give up fruits, vegetables, tofu, and yogurt—I wanted them all the more. Isn't that just human nature? I spent thousands of dollars on personal trainers whose advice I never followed and Flab Master equipment I never used.

The past does not equal the future . . . Have some french fries dipped in mayo.

A short six years ago I even had the reverse lipo-suction procedure, where they pumped fat into me, thinking that was the answer. It was a quick and easy way to gain twenty-five pounds, but complications arose when I kept exercising, and I subsequently lost all the fat pumped into my stomach and thighs in just two months. And guess what? Since my thought process and eating patterns never changed, sixty-five pounds dropped right back off, and thirty more to boot. Even personal accolades of "how great you look in your new Big & Tall suit," were not enough for me to maintain the weight gain. I took a mental beating, day after day, permeating every sinew of my body and all aspects of my life.

Something had to change. I had to take a hard look at myself. Apparently, the fear of gaining weight was much bigger than the actual pain of being thin. What was my fear? How could I be so positive and disciplined in some areas of my life, and so failure-prone regarding my weight?

As I searched inward, over and over, answers began to take form; and results began to take hold. My weight had much more to do with my inner struggle, my tumultuous mindset, than it ever did with the low-calorie food that I put in my mouth.

Throughout this journal, I'm going to share with you some of my innermost thought patterns and struggles, and ask you some pretty tough questions, which you should explore and answer on your journey to gaining weight. Come along in this explorative journey with me for the next thirty days—one day at a time.

When I kept this journal every day, weight gain success came from my focus, and of course eating mass quantities of food. Even when straying from good quality eating, I completed my journal most days, helping me stay committed to change. Come on, journal with me. You'll have nothing to lose, and a lot to gain!

Words of Inspiration

Day One

"You learn to speak by speaking, to study by studying, to walk by walking, to eat by eating, to gain weight by eating abundantly."

– GREG COOK, R.N., ASSOCIATED NURSING FOR THE CLINICALLY THIN

Learning to eat abundantly is key to our program, as well as experiencing the joy of virtual exercising. It sounds so obvious, doesn't it? Consistency and balance in eating rich high-caloric foods in massive amounts was not a habit I developed until recently. Now, most times I don't think before I eat, and enjoy every mouthful. We develop habits, both good and bad, by doing them over and over again. Changing bad habits takes commitment, concentration, and consistency. Don't make a resolution; instead, start a revolution of change from **You Gotta Eat to Win!** within. These next seven days, follow our Seven-Day Quick-Gorge Program, one day at a time. Concentrate on what you want and eliminate all other possibilities. And visualize how good you'll feel with an extra twenty-five pounds in just seven days.

Day Two

"The best time to plant a tree was twenty years ago. The second best time is now. It's never too late to gain weight. Plant an avocado tree, and make some guacamole today."

– CHINESE PROVERB BY DR. NAN KELLY WILSON

This proverb is so profound, and so true. Oftentimes we fret over the missed opportunities in our lives, and let just the thought defeat us, keeping us from moving forward. Okay, so it would have been better to get a handle on gaining weight a year, two years, a decade ago. We've heard it many times before: *There is no time like the present.* Think differently this time around. Begin the process of pursuing change, and being faithful to your commitment to this pursuit. Simply put, your goal needs to be "faithfulness" to abundant eating. Faithfulness is the hallmark to change. Eat my friend, eat.

Day Three

"Isolation is the worst possible counselor. With a raspberry cheesecake, you'll never have to be alone."

– DR. HARRY GLENN, DIRECTOR OF THE KENNEDY FOUNDATION
TO STAMP OUT YOUTH SPORTS

Have you found someone to share your heart with? Have you found someone to share your struggles with? Have you found someone to share your love with? For too long, I lived a secluded life because of being too thin, or should I say because of my fear. Franklin Roosevelt said, "The only thing we have to fear, is fear itself." Fear can lead us to isolation; and isolation can lead us to remaining the same. If you haven't selected three fat accountability support partners, get busy and do it now. You will be so much more successful in your journey of weight gain. Be open. Be vulnerable. Be honest. As thin people we eat too little and exercise too much, and often live in the proverbial closet. We hide. Surrounding yourself with fat people to support you, and for you to support, is a super tonic to reverse the devastation that isolation causes.

Day Four

"Much that I sought, I could not find; Much that I found, I could not bind; Much that I bound, I could not free; Much that I ate, stayed with me."

– JOHN AND LESLEE BRACKIN, ENTHUSIASTICALLY OBESE

Are you at peace with yourself? True peace can be so elusive. Learn to give yourself grace. It took a lifetime to develop the problem of thinness, so in moments of failure, set your heart and mind so that you can turn to a good friend, spouse, or your chubby support partners in the first moments of temptation to not eat and your desire to shut off the television and exert yourself by exercising. Acknowledge your weakness. The concept of asking for help can be difficult to get your arms around and understand—but acknowledge your weakness to others you trust. It's so freeing to be able to call a friend and say: "I'm overwhelmed and feel like jogging right now." A caring friend will ask one simple question: "What's going on?" Get in touch. Be open. Free yourself.

Day Five

"The cart before the horse is neither beautiful nor useful. But dessert before the entrée is wonderful."

– PLATO, RELATED BY LONG-TIME COMPANION JENNIFER HARRIS

I hope that you don't do what I used to do with most programs, by just beginning without reading all the material. Each time I joined a new program I didn't take the time to go through the initiation class or read their material. How smart is that? Here was a quality sensible program right in front of my eyes and I refused to read or follow the material. All I wanted was the weigh-in accountability, to see how much I gained each week. Often I'd go straight to the buffet table while on other programs, and their material would sit in the back seat of my car with the fast food wrappers. That's the ultimate in putting the cart before the horse. So plan on reading every page of our program before beginning. If not, stop right this very moment, get yourself a Big Gulp cola and a bag of chips, and begin to read.

Day Six

"Self-love, my liege, is not so vile a sin as self-neglecting. A soldier should never go to bed on an empty stomach."

– WILLIAM SHAKESPEARE, AS WRITTEN IN THE "TALES OF LINDA MCKINNEY"

The war within is as different as the number of people fighting it, yet for me, for such a long time, I have been unsatisfied. There has been a rage seething from within, that has led me to years of self-neglecting. Before gaining 145 pounds, I had to ask myself: "Am I committed to change? Really? Or is the North Beach Diet just another fad diet?"

If we truly have conviction, we must begin the pattern, or practice, of "putting on." However, before we become practitioners of putting on, we need to become self-detectives. What do we do specifically when we make food choices, such as low-calorie organic fruits and vegetables? What are our thoughts? Why did we think of them? Did we just act out of habit?

What was going on in your mind? You wanted that low-fat yogurt and fresh raspberries, but why? Did you get the urge to eat these foods, and then go find them—or was this food in front of you, and then you got the urge? Search for the answers, and write them out.

Day Seven

"If the wind will not serve, take to the oars. If the soufflé will not rise, take to the pies."

– LATIN PROVERB BY MICHAEL J. O'MALLEY, IRISH PUB OWNER

In your quest to let the real you break through and win the battle of mind over matter, expect a struggle, weariness, and discouragement at times. Sometimes you just won't feel hungry. As you are aware by now, these past six days haven't been a walk in the park . . . excuse me, I mean . . . a piece of cake. Old habits die hard. If we are faithful to our commitment, however, our struggle can be seen as signs of empowerment and overcoming our mental obstacles. Answer these questions in your journal today: What does change look like? How can I remain faithful in the midst of change? Get in touch with what you hate and fear more than gaining weight. Take control of your life by taking the oars and eating the pies.

Day Eight

"To strive, to seek, to find, and not to yield . . . "

– ALFRED LORD TENNYSON, AS TOLD TO BONNIE LEE BAKLEY
ON THE BANKS OF THE SUWANNEE RIVER

This Tennyson quote is one of my favorites. Often, simply repeating it over and over in my mind provides the momentary impetus to continue the path of resisting the temptation of exercise. It's important as well to remove or temper the influences leading you into desiring and repeating addictive behavior. If it's the athletic friends you associate with, or just the habit of taking a long walk after dinner, you must strive to break the ritual patterns of destructive behavior. The remaining stanza of the above Tennyson quote is so beautiful and appropriate: "Tis not too late to seek a newer world. Push off, and sitting well in order smite the sounding furrows, for my purpose holds to sail beyond the sunset, and the baths of all the western stars, until I die." Refuse to submit to the barrage of self-condemning thoughts when you fall. If you've eaten an apple one day, and you feel like you just can't make it, reject the lies of self-hatred, loathing, and shame.

Day Nine

"Look at that word blame. *It's just a coincidence that the last two letters spell the word* me. *But that coincidence is worth thinking about. Other people of unfortunate circumstances may have caused you to feel pain, but only you control whether you allow that pain to go on. If you want those feelings to go away, you have to say: "It's up to me."*

– ARTHUR FREEMAN (NOT SURE WHO HE IS—BUT WE LIKED THE QUOTE)

I went wading in a pool with an overweight friend today. When two women waded into the deep end, I heard one whisper about my friend: "He's a 10," then I heard her say that the skinny one was a "zero." At that moment I decided to take control and gain weight. I went home and ate, starting with dessert.

Do you ever play the "blame" game, and blame someone or something for your poor eating? Bored, lonely, frustrated, sad, happy, an ill-tempered remark, you name it . . . I've used every excuse in the book to pump some iron, jog, or take a bike ride, which only served to maintain the status quo. Get in touch with the triggers and roadblocks that make you remain the same. The woman that made the unkind remark didn't make me thin or want to go running with my awesome dog Sampson—it was me, all me . . . don't kid yourself.

Day Ten

"The Power of One's Mind Is Directly Proportional to the Amount of Food He Eats"

– KYLE OLIPHINT, AUTHOR OF *DEVELOPING A NEEDS-BASED ANIMAL-GESTALT THERAPY FOR YOUR PET*

Is now your time to eat? Is now your time to live? Is now your time to dance? What is it you hate more than being thin? We are selfish enough that when we don't want something, or want something we don't have, we usually do what is needed to get rid of it, or acquire it for ourselves. So why is it then that we find it so difficult to treat our bodies with the respect that we should and to begin eating abundantly? This can be your time to win your never-ending battle to gain weight.

No program or person can do it for you, however. Reflect on what holds you back, on why you are eating too little, and the relationship between your thoughts and acting on them. It's imperative to get in touch with your emotions. *Journal.*

Day Eleven

"I was seldom able to see an opportunity until it ceased to be one. How many times has blueberry pie been placed before me? Yet for some inexplicable self-demented reason, I refused."

– MARK TWAIN, RELATED BY HIS PERSONAL TRAINER JOE GESS

There are so many things we wish we had done yesterday, so few that we feel like doing today. Missed opportunities are part of the fabric of living. They are going to happen. Everywhere we hear *Carpe diem* (seize the day). Instead we should say *Carpe piem* (seize the pie). Nike ads say: "Just Do It!" A few keys to a more balanced approach to taking maximum advantage of this opportunity to gain weight are to 1) develop a specific strategy, 2) identify small measurable steps and set a realistic healthy timeline, 3) commit to changing your lifestyle and yourself, and 4) establish meaningful accountability with those chubby people who will hold your feet to the fire.

Day Twelve

"Achieving success and personal glory in gaining weight has less to do with wins and losses than it does with learning how to prepare yourself, so that at the end of the day, whether at the bakery or at a restaurant, you know that there was nothing more you could have done to reach your ultimate goal."

– NAPOLEON, FRENCH CHEF FOR THE FOREIGN LEGION

Napoleon was so wise. That's why I continue to eat his desserts to this day. The French Napoleon is one of my favorite desserts. The first question people ask me and all people who have gained weight is: "How long did it take?" Stop trying to quantify change and the pace of it, for success and progress should not be measured by how much change has or hasn't taken place. Instead, as we have said over and over, allow your faithfulness to be the barometer in measuring change. In otherwords, don't count the pounds you have gained as the sole evidence of change. Point to the tightening of your belt, pants, or dress as substantiation of a work in progress.

Day Thirteen

Best-selling author Harvey McKay says, "Ideas without action are worthless." Kay Kramer says: "Grits without butter are tasteless."

Use failure as a driving force to succeed. Take an immediate action right now. Write down two life-changing things that you have been putting off, and decide to take immediate action on them. Go ahead! Write them down now.

I've been putting off:

1)_____

2)_____

For example, I had been putting off buying triple extra large T-shirts, and for some reason I was still stocking the fridge with 2 percent milk as opposed to half-and-half or heavy cream. Now I not only have a closet full of XXXL shirts; I buy larger ones as an incentive to grow into them—and my refrigerator is stocked with gallons of heavy cream.

Motivator Anthony Robbins believes that everything we do in life comes from our need to avoid pain and our desire to gain pleasure. He writes, "We will do far more to avoid pain than we will to gain pleasure—pain is a greater motivator."

What actions are you going to take to achieve what you've been putting off?

Action Step One _____

Action Step Two _____

Action Step Three _____

Action Step Four _____

For example, my four action steps were:

1) Have at least one pound of beef jerky each day (it has the added benefit of removing tartar from your teeth).

2) Change all my shoes from laced to slip-on.

3) Purchase a mobile scooter so I'll never have to walk again.

4) Watch infomercials all night long so I can find an in-home job, providing me the super opportunity to be a part of some multi-billion dollar industry.

All my action steps were achieved within thirty days of making a firm commitment to myself. And the best thing is, while watching the infomercial *Travel Perks* starring Robin Leach, I decided to join the multi-billion dollar travel industry as an in-home consultant for cruise lines, allowing me to take advantage of free and discounted cruises worldwide . . . and of course, to eat my way to ultimate nirvana.

Day Fourteen

"You can't leave footprints in the sands of time if you're sitting on your butt. And who wants to leave buttprints in the sands of time?"

– BOB MOAWAD

Who is Bob Moawad anyway? I don't know; I just ran across this quote and thought we could use some humor at the end of week two. How are you doing? Are you remaining faithful to your commitment? Remember, faithful doesn't mean perfection. Last night I ate a plum and a couple of pears for dinner. My day was stressful. Subsequently, I reverted back to old habits and made poor food choices. Then, of all things, I went for a run! I gained control by journaling, and I realized my emotions were being medicated with fruit and exercise. Immediate gratification is so powerful and calming. But the long-term penalty can be tremendous if you don't get quickly in touch.

Day Fifteen

"People become really quite remarkable when they start thinking that they can do things. When they believe in themselves they have the first secret of success."

– NORMAN VINCENT PEALE, AS TOLD TO US
BY HIS AMBIANCE HOSTESS VICKIE GRABER

Last night I wanted to go for a jog. In case you are wondering, jogging is exercise. In place of jogging, my urge was to go to a counterfeit—walking or swimming. Instead I e-mailed my overweight accountability partner about my exercise quest and need to exert energy. He simply wrote, "Why exercise?" Then he continued, "Think hard about that question. Journal and figure out: What is up there? What is it about exercise that makes you tick? Why do you crave it? How do you view it? What role does not having it play in your life? How do you view others in light of exercise? Do you have every one in nice, clean categories and think, 'Well, they enjoy exercise whenever they want.'? How much of this exercise thing do you allow to define you? How does going for a run affect your long-term weight gain goals?"

What great searching questions! He didn't coddle me—he pointed me in the direction of getting emotionally in touch. In the past, however, I'd keep quiet about my emotions for fear of not looking strong. Look what great counsel I'd have missed. Openness, confession, and vulnerability will breed success!

Day Sixteen

"The last of the human freedoms—to choose one's attitude in any given set of circumstances, to choose one's own way."

– VICTOR FRANKL, AUTHOR OF *MAN'S SEARCH FOR MEANING*

If you see the same, you will be the same. Victor Frankl was a proponent of visualization. If you don't visualize success, you won't ever get there. Remember too that life's decisions are made in your heart, and it's important to move toward (not away from) a decision or action.

If you move away, when the pain lessens, you can get sucked back into the same self-destructive patterns of eating natural foods and unsauced vegetables. We are totally responsible for our state of mind. If you are driving down the road and someone cuts in front of you and flips you the finger—it's solely in your control how you deal with this. Do you flip him back? Does it ruin your day? It's up to you. The same goes for daily stresses in your life.

Will you eat a fresh mango as a consequence of stress? For most of us the state we are in determines our behavior and performance. Dr. Andrew Weil suggests that we close our eyes and take several deep breaths—holding each one for at least five to ten seconds. We suggest that you hold your breath with a mouth full of Häagen-Dazs cookies and cream ice cream. It works.

Day Seventeen

"The desire accomplished is like sweet peach cobbler to the soul."
– KEN GIORDANO, GEORGIA PEACH FARMER

My desire for tofu burgers and sprouts often has been more emotionally based than to satisfy a hunger pang. It has helped me greatly to understand what my real desires are so I can get in touch with the emotion(s) of the moment. Late last night I became frustrated when a friend did not come over for some binge eating. I was really looking forward to getting together, and she didn't call until two hours after she said she would visit, which made me mad. Immediately upon hanging up, I had an insatiable desire to go for a bike ride. At midnight, my sole desire was to go to the track and exert some energy. Instead, I turned on the TV, sat down with a box of Little Debbie Oatmeal Snack Cakes and got in touch with my true desires. Crisis was averted . . . today. Be assured, however, other negative desires will arise, yet it was such a sweet feeling to wake up this morning, stuffed from the night before. Mission accomplished.

Day Eighteen

Well-known motivational speaker Zig Ziglar says, "You can have everything in life you want, if you just help enough other people get what they want."

Regina Beck says, "You can have everything in life you want, if you just help enough other people get what they want to eat."

When I began to grasp this Zig Ziglar thought process it helped me become a bit less preoccupied with myself. Let's face it. We are a self-centered bunch. Oprah Winfrey started a great campaign a few years back, suggesting that we pass on daily "acts of kindness."

The feeling I had paying for the person's food behind me at the Burger King drive-through, was, to put it mildly . . . fun. It made me laugh and made my day. Give someone a piece of cherry pie today. Smile. Give a caregiver a day off and a gift certificate to a local all-you-can-eat buffet. Work in the local soup kitchen a few weekends a year.

Bring a dozen Krispy Kreme hot glazed donuts to someone you haven't spoken to in years. The list is endless. Focus on others, and it will come back many fold. Giving food to others will help you feel alive. The second-best chef in all of America, Patricia Anderson, said, "Food is love made visible."

Day Nineteen

> *"Sow an act and you reap a habit.*
> *Sow a habit and you reap a character.*
> *Sow a character and you reap a destiny.*
> *Eat a pie, and you'll need to sew your pants."*
>
> — SYLVIA DIPRONIO PERKINS, PRIZED BELLY
> BUMPING CHAMPION—DISNEY ON PARADE

Do something today and the next ten days to build a habit. Hopefully you've been eating huge amounts at breakfast every morning. If not, start today. Hopefully, you've been vegging out in front of the TV every night. If not, start today. Maybe take an extra portion of oven-roasted garlic mashed potatoes at dinner. Maybe turn the TV off after 1:00 A.M. and talk with your family or a friend, or write in your journal.

Pay attention to your habits, both the positive and negative ones. When the phone rang, my best friend used to pick up a chocolate Moon Pie and an RC Cola. When I sat in front of the TV at nights, I used to eat apples and celery stalks; now I eat sweets and chips. Doing something different, something positive, helps create a habit that can last a lifetime. If I hadn't stopped eating fruit late at night, my destiny would have been to never enjoy the true crunch a mesquite barbeque chip has to offer, thus not attaining my life's goals. Pay attention to your habits, for if you change your habits you will change your character, and then your destiny.

Day Twenty

> *"Accept what you are able to do and what you are not able to do. Accept the past as past, without denying it or discarding it. Learn to forgive yourself and to forgive others. Don't assume that it's too late to get involved."*
>
> — MORRIE SCHWARTZ, FROM *TUESDAYS WITH MORRIE*

"If only I gained my weight when I was twenty." "If only I wore a size 56 pants." If only . . . if only . . . if only. We can "if only" ourselves to death and subsequently remain the same year after year. If change is on your horizon, you must first identify what you want to change; and link enough pain to your present habit so your brain wants to move as far away from it as possible. Then, identify a new desire or belief and heap as much pleasure to it as possible.

For example, I hated being thin. So I wrote down every negative association with my gaunt look as possible. There were literally hundreds of things I kept myself from doing in my lifetime because I was six feet tall and weighed 175. Not anymore. Now, write down the pleasure you'll receive by achieving your weight-gain goals. Keep these two lists with you at all times—review them daily, or at least each time you stray to an artificial sweetener.

Day Twenty-One

"For now, recognize that your payoff is often that you feel safe when you don't attempt change, and threatened when you do."

– DR. PHILLIP MCGRAW, AUTHOR OF *LIFE STRATEGIES*

While we are concerned that Dr. Phil has written a best-selling diet book promoting losing weight, *The Ultimate Weight Loss Solution*, given our sense of fair play, and because he remains a bit thick around the middle himself, we have included the above quote.

It took me a long time to realize just how safe I felt staying the same thin weight. It can be very scary to change; at least it was (and sometimes remains so) for me. On March 4, 1933, during his first inaugural address, Franklin Roosevelt stood at the United States Capitol and said: "The only thing we have to fear, is fear itself." Truer words were never spoken, well, that might be an exaggeration—maybe Marie Antoinette's words: "Let them eat cake," but that's off the subject.

Change for me was to discover how to love and respect myself more than playing basketball at the gym every day. When tempted, we need to ask ourselves, "What do I love right now—playing sandlot ball, or myself?" So often exercise is a counterfeit to intimacy, friends, family, love, or fun. It has been for me. When we participate in sports to subjugate some emotion, or to replace something, it works for the moment. It can serve us well in that instant. Yet it does not last. Invite those same guys you play ball with to join you in a fun game of Spin the Bucket with Little Debbie Snack Cakes or even a Nathan's Hot Dog Eating Contest—there is no better way to bond with good friends.

Day Twenty-Two

"Success is the ability to go from one failure to another with no loss of enthusiasm. To go from one drink to another without stumbling. To go from one shepherd's pie to another without bloating."

– WINSTON CHURCHILL

Good ole Winston knew how to eat . . . we just love him.

Just got off the phone with a good friend, internationally self-proclaimed expert on dealing directly with the obese, David E. Ward. He's never had a weight problem and maintains his ideal weight of 368 pounds by what he calls "chowing down." When he eats a big lunch he has an even bigger dinner. If he eats heavy all day, he spends the next day enjoying all his meals lying on the couch.

When he and his wife Linda went on a three-week vacation throughout France, with overweight country and western stars Lyle and Brenda Charles, they enjoyed lots of rich decadent food. He struggled with having gained only seven pounds. "I walked too much," he said wistfully. Upon his return, he spent long lunch hours at a local "salad bar" restaurant, which is a great place to pack on extra pounds. It worked! He gained ten additional pounds in just two weeks.

Against our advice, he weighs every day when at home. However, no friend of mine loves and enjoys food the way this guy does. And we believe he will eat up to a 400-pound girth in no time. He has as much passion for food as any person I know. He truly lives to eat. His mindset is right on target, and he does what works for him. His goal is to "eat hardy and don't exercise." He's got it down because he knows his goal and has worked it to the point of becoming a habit.

Day Twenty-Three

"Let the little things go. We have in common that we're on this planet for a relatively short time. If we can't love each other, then let's at least give each other a break. Everyone is having a harder time than it appears."

– CHARLES GRODIN, AUTHOR OF *HOW I GET THROUGH LIFE*

There's a good book out there: *Don't Sweat The Small Stuff*, with the subtitle: *And Remember, It's All Small Stuff*. What kind of a day are you having today? Are you in control? Or are you letting someone else affect how you feel? Did little Johnny throw a tantrum at the grocery because you made a mistake and didn't let him have everything he wanted? Does feeling out of control affect the way you eat? It does me, and in the past I'd often just lose my appetite.

Now I reach for some kind of sweet carbohydrate like a doughnut or piece of cake. Okay, okay, doughnuts, plural, or an entire cake. Spice cake with a rich butter-cream icing and a couple of scoops of cinnamon applesauce ice cream that glides down the palate like a velvet stole over a starlet's shoulders—wait a minute . . . wait a minute—sorry about that, folks. I just got off on a food tangent. See how easy it is on the North Beach Diet? The bottom line is that we've got to rise above the magnetic pull of our Reeboks and stay in control of how we deal with our emotions. Make it a good day today. Eat through your emotions. It is your choice.

Day Twenty-Four

"The only time you don't fail is the time you try anything and it works."
– ROOFER DOUG SHIELDS

Keep trying. Those are easier words to say than to follow. How do we keep trying when we've failed so often? Procrastination has been my nemesis. Do you put things off until they become critical? Answer this question: *If I don't eat an abundance of food today, what's going to be the ultimate price I'll have to pay?* Then ask yourself: *If I'd already gained the weight I wanted to, how would my life be better? How much more joy would I have?*

Now list three negative emotions you experience often (depression, discouragement, and sadness, for example). Next list three positive emotions you experience often, then write down what happens in your mind when you experience these emotions. My negative emotions can keep me in my procrastination mode, so the key is to find ways to interrupt the negative. Saying things to yourself such as "I want to . . ." instead of "I have to . . . " helps a great deal, as does being around other overweight people, or going for a banana split or a box of Dunkin' Donuts. Next time you are in a funk, get in your car and drive to

Baskin-Robbins—order scoops of all twenty-eight flavors . . . begin to associate ice cream with breaking your negative patterns.

Day Twenty-Five

"Most of us are just about as happy as we make up our minds to be. You can have anything you want if you want it badly enough. You can be anything you want to be, do anything you set out to accomplish if you hold to that desire with singleness of purpose. Many are afraid to have their cake and eat it too— go ahead, have no fear."

— ABRAHAM LINCOLN

Before Abraham Lincoln became president he failed at just about everything he attempted, from business to running for Congress—he even failed at gaining weight. He did succeed at never giving up, however. It was reported by the then White House chief nurse, Jamie Atkinson, that Lincoln had to be treated for malnourishment. Apparently Mr. Lincoln was notorious for refusing food, maintaining his gaunt state throughout his presidency.

When the secret service agent saw John Wilkes Booth lunge toward the President, he yelled for Mr. Lincoln to "duck." Apparently, Lincoln thought the agent was offering duck—so he turned to the agent and said politely, "No, thank you, just don't feel like any duck tonight." At that sad moment, Mr. Lincoln was shot. The course of history would have been changed if the secret service agent had only said "move" instead of duck. For that very reason—to this day—duck has never been served at White House functions, even when the Mayor of Peking was honored at a state dinner.

Let me ask you, and be honest with me and more importantly, honest with yourself: "Do you want to gain weight enough to change your habit or belief system?" We've become masters at deceiving ourselves (self-deception), and sometimes we simply refuse to listen to sound advice (rebellion). What are the habits keeping you from achieving the success you dream about? Write down just two. Close your eyes and think about the consequences, both past and present, that you've experienced because of these habits. Put yourself five years into the future, then ten and twenty years—what will be the cost for maintaining these habits? The thin lead miserable lives—they are always counting carbs, fat grams, and calories. What kind of existence is that?

Day Twenty-Six

"Everything is kneaded out of the same dough but not baked in the same oven."

— YIDDISH PROVERB BY MAHATMA GANDHI

Stephen Covey suggests that we write out various eulogies we would like people to say about us at our funeral. What would you like your spouse, child, best friend, or coworker to say about you when you die? Be specific. His thought process is to begin with the end in mind. If, for example, you would love to hear your child say that you were a loving parent with a zest for cooking—how can you now begin living your life to fulfill that quest?

We all know that we are going to die, but how would you live differently if you knew that death was two years from today? I'd go to cooking school for a year in France, and cook huge meals for my family and friends the last year. Morrie Schwartz suggests that we pretend to have a little bird on our shoulders, asking it daily: Is today the day? Am I ready? Am I doing all I need to do? Am I being the person I want to be? Have I eaten all I can today? Answer these five questions in your journal.

Day Twenty-Seven

"Being defeated is often a temporary condition. Giving up is what makes it permanent."

— MARILYN VOS SAVANT

What do you do when temptation arises? As a former child athlete, temptation for me comes from many corners in the sports arena. It can be as simple as being invited to a football game or my neighbor's daughter's track meet. Literally any kind of sporting event used to trigger the desire to work out. Thankfully, there are many food purveyors at all stadiums that make it easy to stick to our program. I've trained myself to never take a seat at a public sporting event before getting a large coke, loaded chili dog, buttered popcorn, and a couple of Snickers. More often than not, constant snacking keeps the temptation to exercise away.

Sometimes, misguided thin people will watch me eating and make a comment such as "Should you be eating that?" Instead of getting angry, befriend these people—they need to eat, too. You'd be shocked at how many times I went to a football or baseball game and ate nothing out of fear of someone making an unkind remark about how thin I was. Now, because of my newfound girth and sense of pride, I embrace these remarks as a way to make new friends. The first thing I do is invite them to Steak & Shake after the game for a double cheeseburger, large fries and onion rings, and a chocolate shake—all eaten in the car.

Now, I plan my potential temptations and take action steps to avoid these pitfalls. It's important too, to enjoy both the company and the food, but if given only one of the two, I choose the food, every time. And remember to bring a bag of Brach's chocolate covered peanuts to every game just in case you have an opportunity to make a new friend.

Day Twenty-Eight

"Failure is the opportunity to begin again more intelligently."

– HENRY FORD

Inevitably you are going to fall off the wagon by eating some low-carb snack. It's okay—don't beat yourself up. Sometimes events trigger poor eating, and sometimes people do.

At church tonight a little girl standing eye level to my stomach said, "Little tummy." I was dumbfounded by her comment. I had been trying so hard to gain weight. I think it was the navy blue pants I was wearing, because they always make me look slimmer. This little girl's father, a friend, was horrified because he knew how much time I'd been putting into my weight gain program. He looked at her sternly and said, "Now, Cynthia, you know better than to say a thing like that." I immediately picked up brownies in both hands and began to let everyone know I was still committed to my regimen.

At that point in the program I had only gained 100 pounds of the 145 I wanted to gain, so I was feeling a bit anxious. Sometimes I think that I'm looking good, then reality hits. Before I go out, I look in the mirror, stick out my stomach, turning from side to side, figuring what angle is best. Well, there is no angle to hide a need of forty-five pounds. I'm still thin in everyone's book, including my own.

157

I must have thought about this little girl's comments a dozen times already. Even though I wasn't hungry, I ordered a large pizza and ate half of it on the way home. I stayed up eating most of the night. Yes, I got a grip on my emotions. I'm beginning to use these comments to propel me to keep my focus and commitment. I'm not completely there yet, but I didn't go to the gym either. That's success.

Day Twenty-Nine

"There is no try . . . only do, or do not."

– YODA, *STAR WARS* MOVIE CHARACTER

The Marines have but one answer a recruit may give when a drill sergeant asks a question regarding some mishap: "Sir, no excuses, sir!" Even if the recruit had nothing to do the problem. Similarly, you must always give the same answer if you go off your eating plan for whatever reason. Recently, a friend who wants to gain about sixty pounds committed to eat a half-gallon of ice cream every evening after dinner. The first week she stuck to her commitment every day without a hitch. Week two she missed two days. Week three, she missed *four* days. Now she no longer eats ice cream. There was always an excuse, and many of them were valid. But she was stumped when I asked why she couldn't eat ice cream in the morning, at lunch, or figure out some other time. Her mentality is not foreign to me, for I was there most of my life. Now's the time to be different. Are you going to do what it takes to achieve your goal without excuses? Be honest with yourself.

Day Thirty

"Most of what I really need to know about how to live and what to do and how to be I learned in kindergarten. Wisdom was not at the top of the graduate-school mountain, but there in the sandpile at Sunday school. These are the things I learned: Share everything. Play fair. Don't hit people. Put things back where you found them. Clean up your mess. Don't take things that aren't yours. Say you're sorry when you hurt somebody. Wash your hands before you eat. Flush. Warm cookies and cold milk are good for you. Live a balanced life—learn some and think some and draw and paint and sing and dance and play and work every day some. Take a nap every afternoon. When you go out into the

world, watch out for traffic, hold hands, and stick together. Above all, be aware of wonder."

– Robert Fulghum, author of *All I Really Need To Know I Learned In Kindergarten*

I can't improve on that one bit. Enjoy life's journey. Keep your commitment to your commitment, and we will all see each other at heaven's little burger stand in the sky. Faith. Peace. Laugh. Take care of yourself.

INDEX

A

Apple Crisp, 59
Apple Date Cake, 64
Aunt Hilda's Blueberry Cake Recipe, 66
Authentic Louisiana Red Beans
  and Rice, 87
Authentic Swiss Fondue, 115

B

Bacon Rice and Beans, 99
Battered Fried Twinkies, 41
Beef
  Best Darn Meatloaf in America, 108
  Cognac-Braised Short Ribs, 114–115
  Easy Slow-Cooked Brisket Pot Roast, 118
  Hamburgers to Die for, 106
  Italian Meatballs, 109
  Pan Seared Rib-Eye Steak, 104
Beer-Battered Deep-Fried Snickers, 42
Bern's King Midas Carrot Cake, 51
Best Chocolate Ice Cream, the, 63
Best Darn Meatloaf in America, 108
Best Tastin' Salsa on Earth, the, 95
Better-Than-Old-Fashioned
  Banana Cake, 74
Biscuits and Chocolate Gravy, 84–85
Breakfast for Dinner, 100
Buttermilk Vidalia Onion Rings, 103
Buttery Corn on the Cob, 86

C

Cakes
  Apple Date Cake, 64
  Aunt Hilda's Blueberry Cake
    Recipe, 66
  Bern's King Midas Carrot Cake, 51
  Better-Than-Old-Fashioned Banana
    Cake, 74
  Finest Cheesecake You'll Ever Taste,
    the, 58

  Medicinal Chocolate Cake, 39
  Spanish Bar Cakes, 65
  Sumptuous Carrot Cake, 50–51
Caramelized Onion Relish, 117
Cheddar Cheesy Hash Browns with Sour
  Cream, 90
Cheese Dishes
  Authentic Swiss Fondue, 115
  Cheddar Cheesy Hash Browns with
    Sour Cream, 90
  Darn Good Quiche, 96–97
  Gorgonzola and Balsamic Portabella
    Mushroom Potato Salad, 91
  Maytag Blue Cheese Mashed
    Potatoes, 101
  Quick and Easy Macaroni and
    Cheese, 111
Cognac-Braised Short Ribs, 114–115
Cookies
  Faux Neiman-Marcus Cookie, the, 48
  Mom's Midnight Snack Sugar
    Cookies, 47
Corn Casserole, 86
Cracked Wheat Bread, 81

D

Darn Good Quiche, 96–97
Delicious New England Corn
  Chowder, 89
Dessert Pies
  Flossie's Best-Ever Pumpkin Pie, 70–71
  Lemon Meringue Pie, 52–53
  Mark Merrill Sweet Potato Pie, the, 44
  McDonald's Hot Apple Pie à la
    Mode, 45
  Southern Pecan Pie, 67
  Whoopi Pies, 60
Desserts
  Apple Crisp, 59
  Apple Date Cake, 64

INDEX

Aunt Hilda's Blueberry Cake
Recipe, 66

Battered Fried Twinkies, 41

Beer-Battered Deep-Fried Snickers, 42

Bern's King Midas Carrot Cake, 51

Best Chocolate Ice Cream, the, 63

Better-Than-Old-Fashioned Banana
Cake, 74

Double Sucked and Filled Jelly
Donuts, 56

Faux Neiman-Marcus Cookie, the, 48

Finest Cheesecake You'll Ever Taste,
the, 58

Flossie's Best-Ever Pumpkin Pie, 70–71

French Market Beignets
(Doughnuts), 75

Homemade Country-Style Vanilla Ice
Cream, 61

Lemon Meringue Pie, 52–53

Mark Merrill Sweet Potato Pie, the, 44

McDonald's Hot Apple Pie à la
Mode, 45

Medicinal Chocolate Cake, 39

Mom's Midnight Snack Sugar
Cookies, 47

Most Delicious Brownie You'll Ever
Eat, the, 54

New Orleans Bread Pudding with
Whiskey Icing, 72–73

OLN Trail Mix Recipe, the, 57

Orange and Chocolate Chip Cookie
Ice Cream, 62

Purple Cow, the, 68

7-Layer Nabisco English Trifle, 69

Southern Pecan Pie, 67

Spanish Bar Cakes, 65

"Spin the Bucket" With Little
Debbie, 55

Sumptuous Carrot Cake, 50–51

Wendy's Chocolate Frosty Smash, 46

Whoopi Pies, 60

Double Sucked and Filled Jelly Donuts, 56

E

Easy Slow-Cooked Brisket Pot Roast, 118

F

Faux Neiman-Marcus Cookie, the, 48

Finest Cheesecake You'll Ever Taste, the, 58

Flossie's Best-Ever Pumpkin Pie, 70–71

French Market Beignets (Doughnuts), 75

Fried Pork Chops with Velveeta Cheese
Sauce, 102

G

Gorgonzola and Balsamic Portabella
Mushroom Potato Salad, 91

H

Ham and Potato Hash, 101

Hamburgers to Die for, 106

Homemade Country-Style Vanilla Ice
Cream, 61

I

Ice Cream
Bern's King Midas Carrot Cake, 51
Best Chocolate Ice Cream, the, 63
Double Sucked and Filled Jelly
Donuts, 56
Homemade Country-Style Vanilla Ice
Cream, 61
McDonald's Hot Apple Pie à la
Mode, 45
Orange and Chocolate Chip Cookie
Ice Cream, 62
Purple Cow, the, 68
Wendy's Chocolate Frosty Smash, 46

Incredible Marinara Sauce, 110

Italian Meatballs, 109

J

Jalapeño Wrap, 78

L

Lemon Meringue Pie, 52–53

M

Main Courses
Authentic Swiss Fondue, 115
Bacon Rice and Beans, 99

Best Darn Meatloaf in America, 108
Breakfast for Dinner, 100
Buttermilk Vidalia Onion Rings, 103
Cognac-Braised Short Ribs, 114–115
Easy Slow-Cooked Brisket Pot
  Roast, 118
Fried Pork Chops with Velveeta
  Cheese Sauce, 102
Ham and Potato Hash, 101
Hamburgers to Die For, 106
Incredible Marinara Sauce, 110
Italian Meatballs, 109
Maytag Blue Cheese Mashed
  Potatoes, 101
Pan Seared Rib-Eye Steak, 104
Pulled Pork Butt so Good, You'll
  Wanna Kick Yourself, 116
Quick and Easy Macaroni and
  Cheese, 111
Really Good and Really Easy
  Homemade Chicken Pot Pie,
  112–113
Vodka Pasta, 102–103
Mark Merrill Sweet Potato Pie, the, 44
Maytag Blue Cheese Mashed Potatoes, 101
McDonald's Hot Apple Pie à la Mode, 45
Medicinal Chocolate Cake, 39
Mom's Midnight Snack Sugar Cookies, 47
Most Delicious Brownie You'll Ever Eat,
  the, 54

N
New Orleans Bread Pudding with
  Whiskey Icing, 72–73

O
OLN Trail Mix Recipe, the, 57
Orange and Chocolate Chip Cookie Ice
  Cream, 62
Overstuffed Twice Baked Potatoes, 93

P
Pan Seared Rib-Eye Steak, 104
Potato Chip and Miracle Whip
  Sandwich, 79

Potatoes
  Cheddar Cheesy Hash Browns with
    Sour Cream, 90
  Gorgonzola and Balsamic Portabella
    Mushroom Potato Salad, 91
  Ham and Potato Hash, 101
  Maytag Blue Cheese Mashed
    Potatoes, 101
  Overstuffed Twice Baked Potatoes, 93
  Stupendously Delicious Scalloped
    Potatoes, 94
  Tasty Dip for French Fries, a , 92
Pulled Pork Butt so Good, You'll Wanna
  Kick Yourself, 116
Purple Cow, the, 68

Q
Quick and Easy Macaroni and Cheese, 111

R
Really Good and Really Easy Homemade
  Chicken Pot Pie, 112–113

S
Sandwiches
  Cracked Wheat Bread, 81
  Jalapeño Wrap, 78
  Potato Chip and Miracle Whip
    Sandwich, 79
  Spam and Pork and Bean Focaccia, 77
  Triple-Decker Mama Cass Elliot Ham
    Sandwich, 80
7-Layer Nabisco English Trifle, 69
Southern Pecan Pie, 67
Spam and Pork and Bean Focaccia, 77
Spanish Bar Cakes, 65
"Spin the Bucket" With Little Debbie, 55
Stupendously Delicious Scalloped
  Potatoes, 94
Sumptuous Carrot Cake, 50–51

T
Tasty Dip for French Fries, a, 92
Triple-Decker Mama Cass Elliot Ham
  Sandwich, 80

INDEX

U

Ultimate Fried Anything, the, 117

V

Vegetables
  Authentic Louisiana Red Beans and
    Rice, 87
  Best Tastin' Salsa on Earth, the, 95
  Biscuits and Chocolate Gravy, 84–85
  Buttermilk Vidalia Onion Rings, 103
  Buttery Corn on the Cob, 86
  Caramelized Onion Relish, 117
  Cheddar Cheesy Hash Browns with
    Sour Cream, 90
  Corn Casserole, 86
  Darn Good Quiche, 96–97
  Delicious New England Corn
    Chowder, 89

Gorgonzola and Balsamic Portabella
    Mushroom Potato Salad, 91
  Maytag Blue Cheese Mashed
    Potatoes, 101
  Overstuffed Twice Baked Potatoes, 93
  Stupendously Delicious Scalloped
    Potatoes, 94
  Tasty Dip for French Fries, a, 92
  Yellow Squash Casserole, 98
Vodka Pasta, 102–103

W

Wendy's Chocolate Frosty Smash, 46
Whoopi Pies, 60

Y

Yellow Squash Casserole, 98

ABOUT THE AUTHOR

KIM BAILEY has written many corporate manuals on marketing, management, and operations for seminars he conducts. *The North Beach Diet* is his first published book. Kim has struggled with weight just about all his life, and is poking gentle fun at both himself and the advertising approaches of the diet industry, which he knows intimately.

Kim has cooked and entertained all of his life, and has provided some of his favorite recipes for you to enjoy with your friends and family. He speaks fluent French Cuisine, and resides in Tampa, Florida, surrounded by many fine restaurants. He loves all food, from gourmet to meat and three.

For humorous or motivational keynote speeches or corporate seminars on marketing, management, and operations, please visit Kim's Web site or email him.

www.northbeachdietonline.com
RobertKimBailey@hotmail.com